BOOK OF GUYS

PETER SLATER

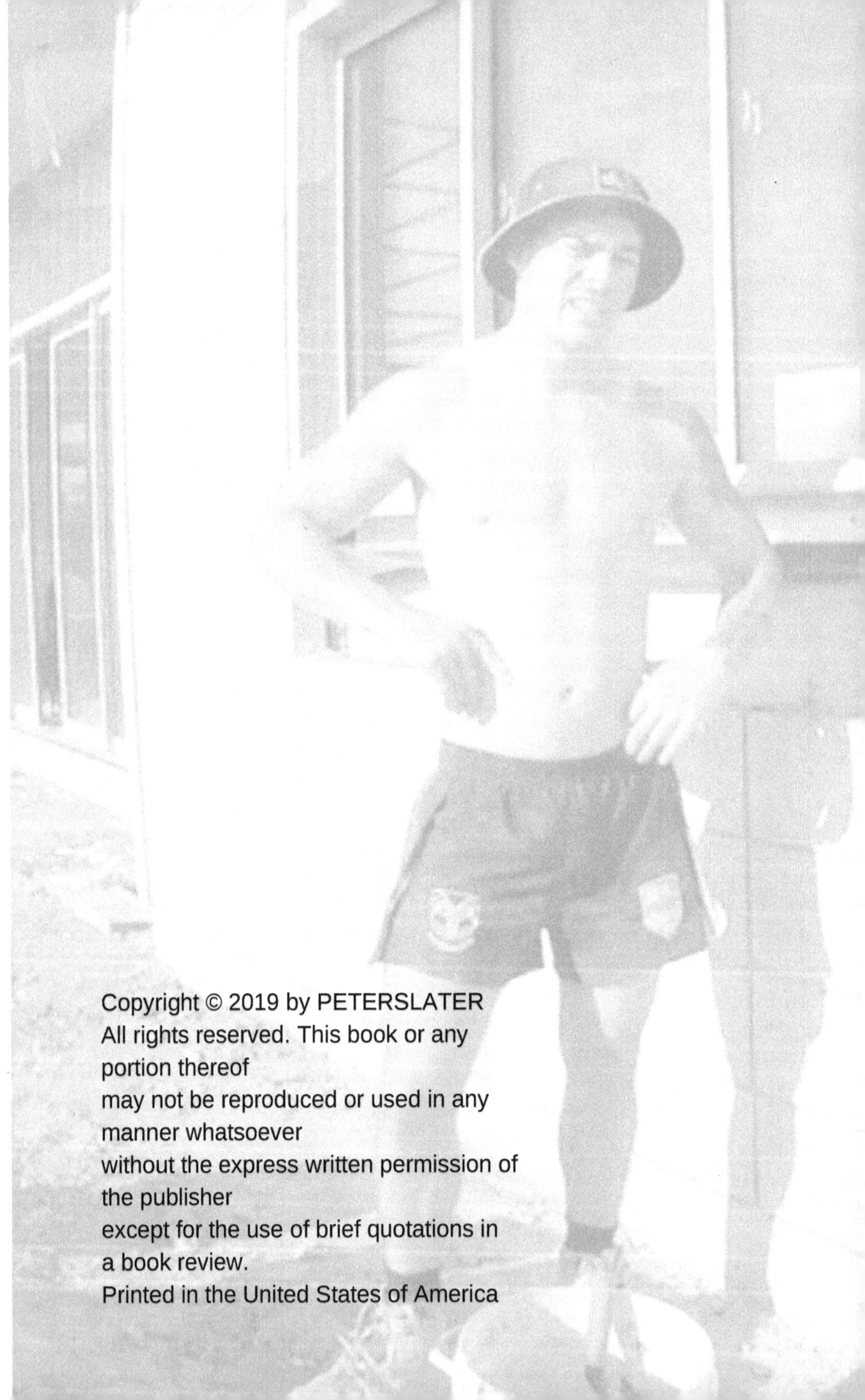

"IF YOU ARE GOING TO BE A CHAMPION, YOU MUST BE WILLING TO PAY A GREATER PRICE"

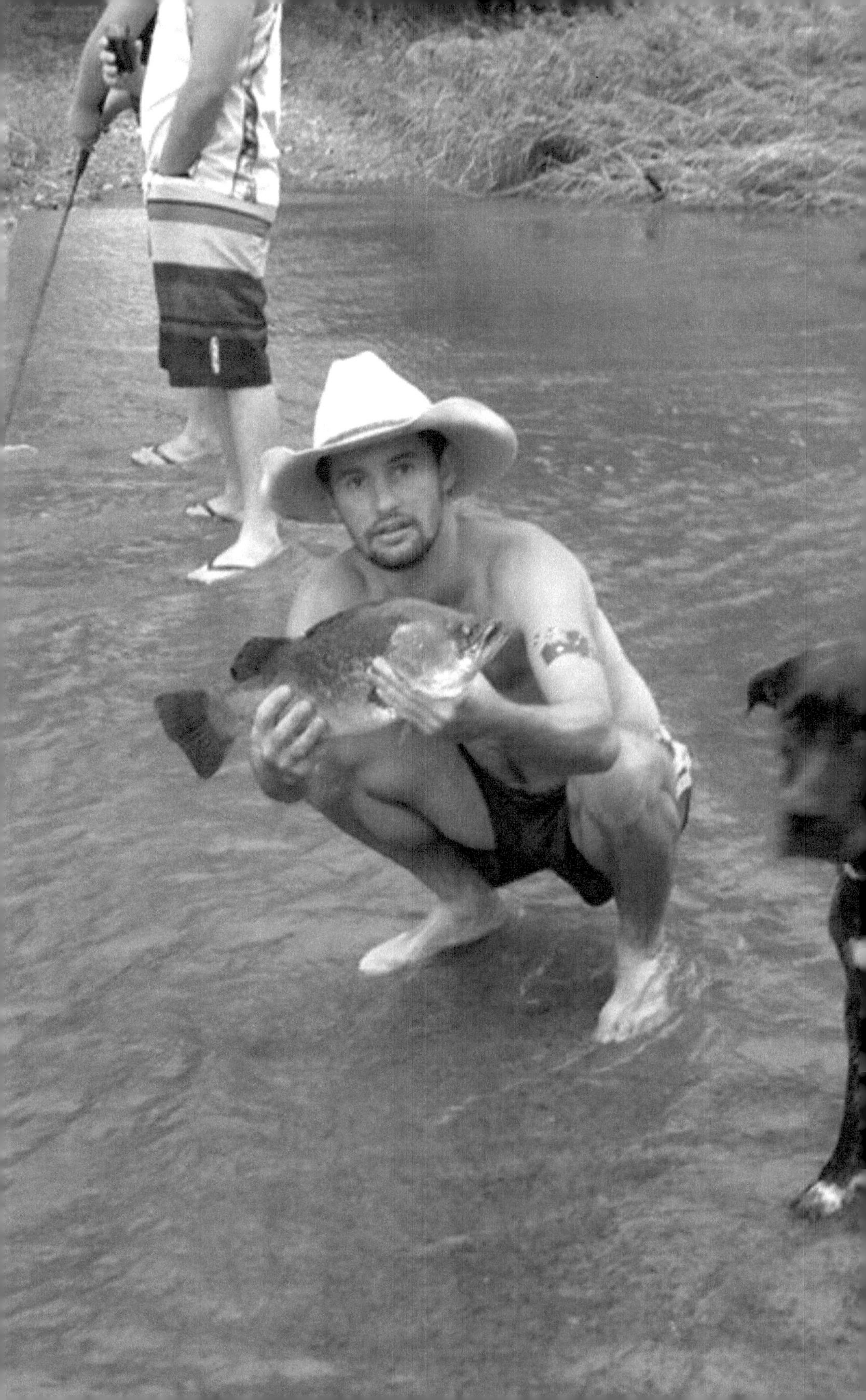

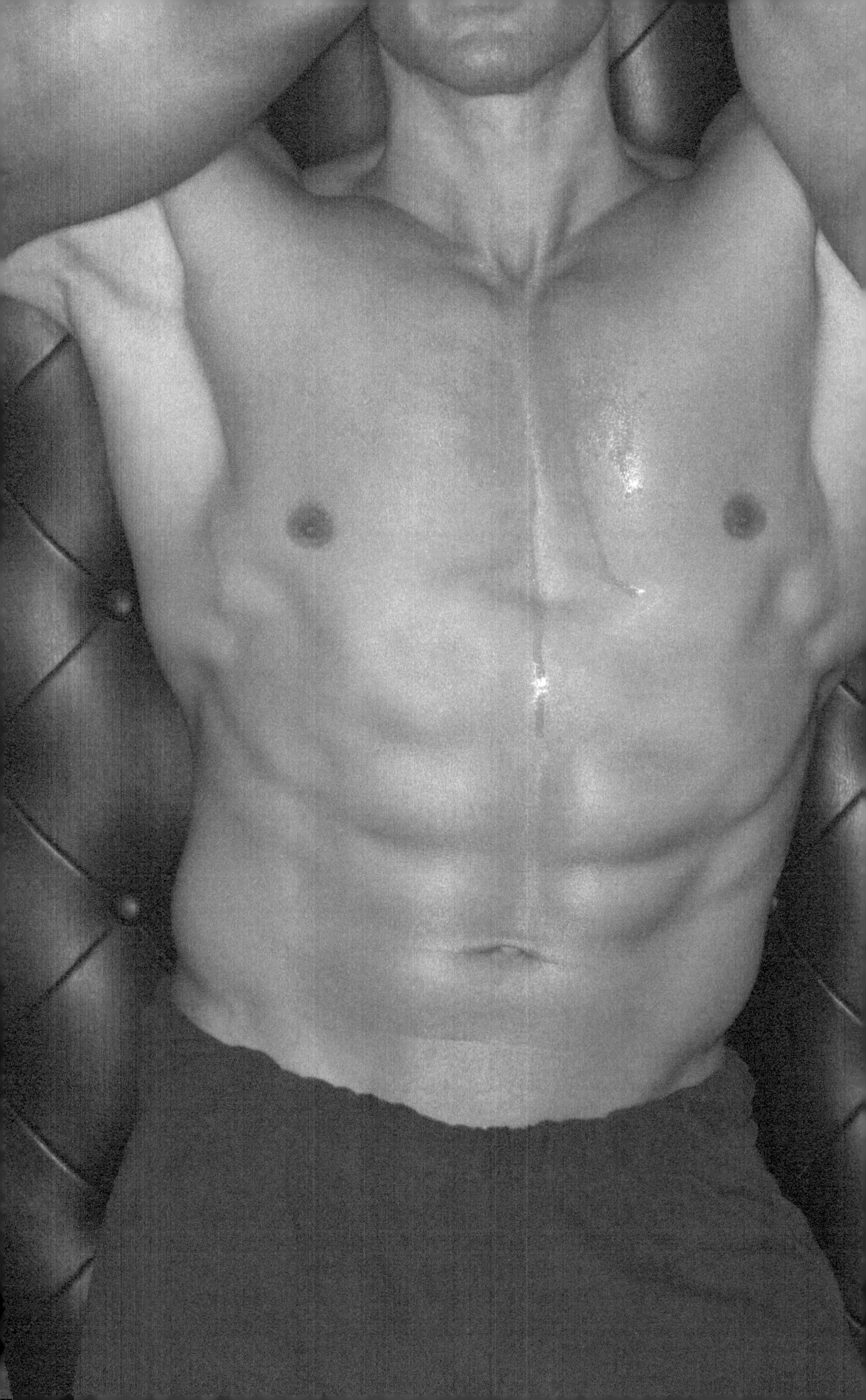

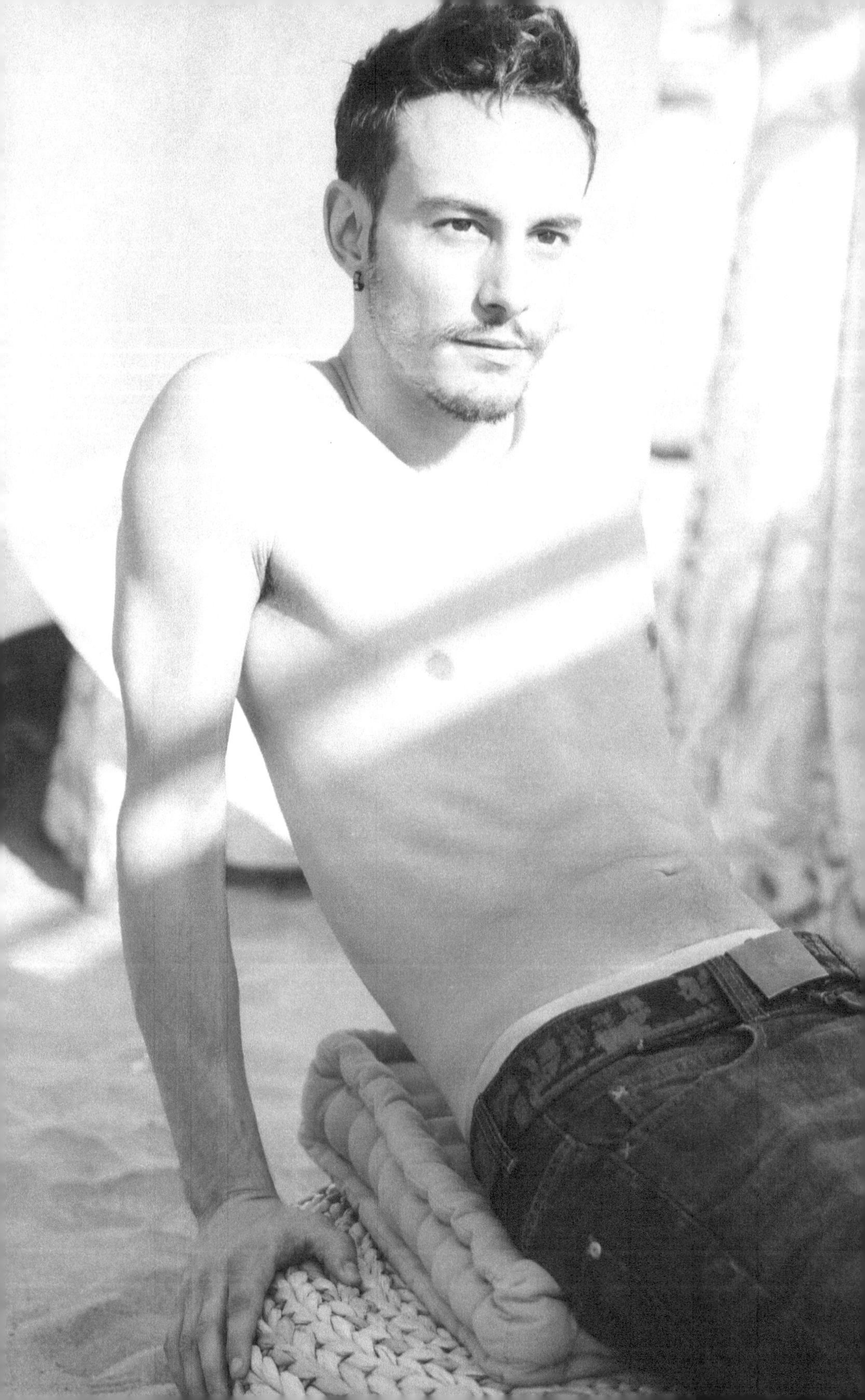

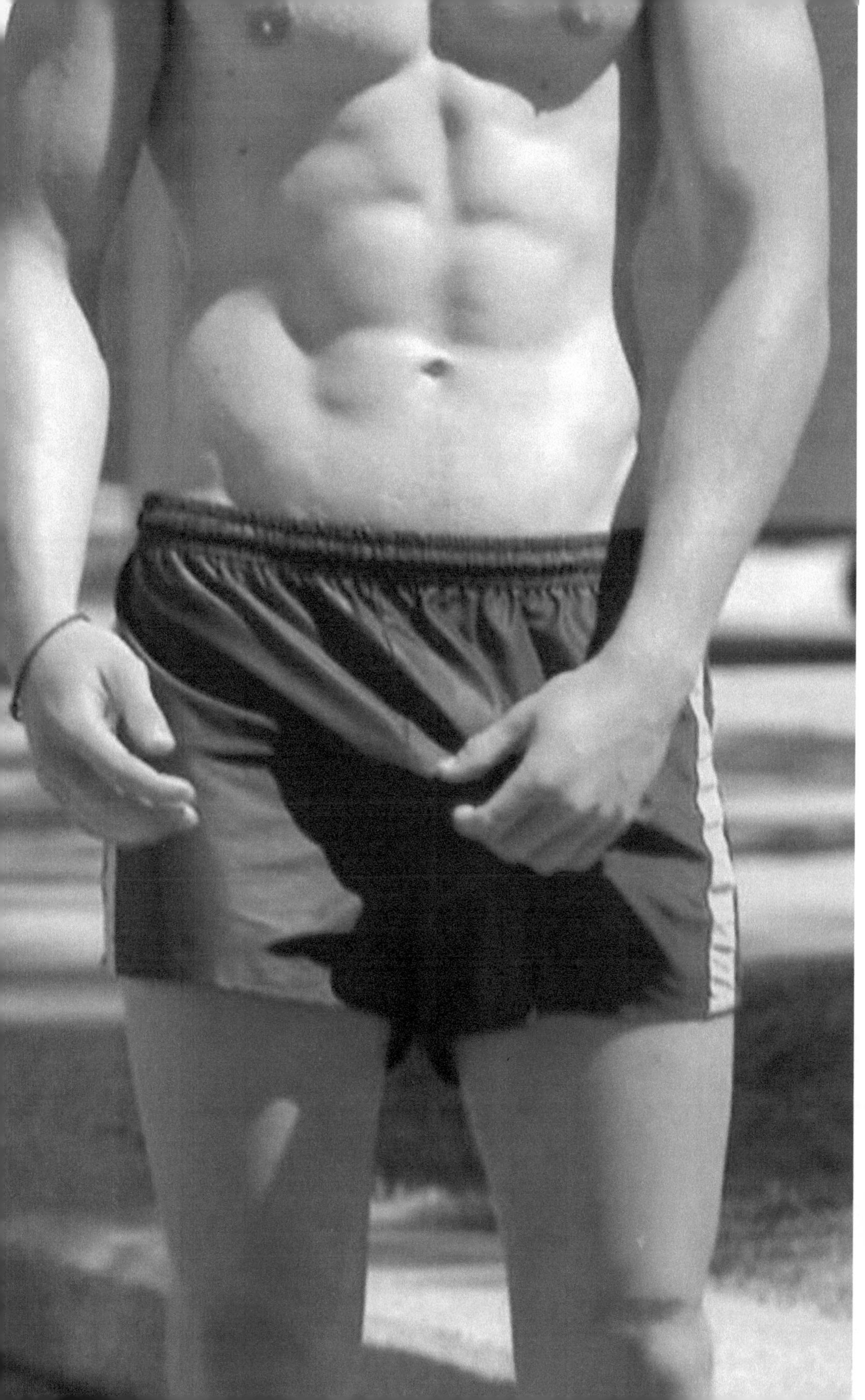

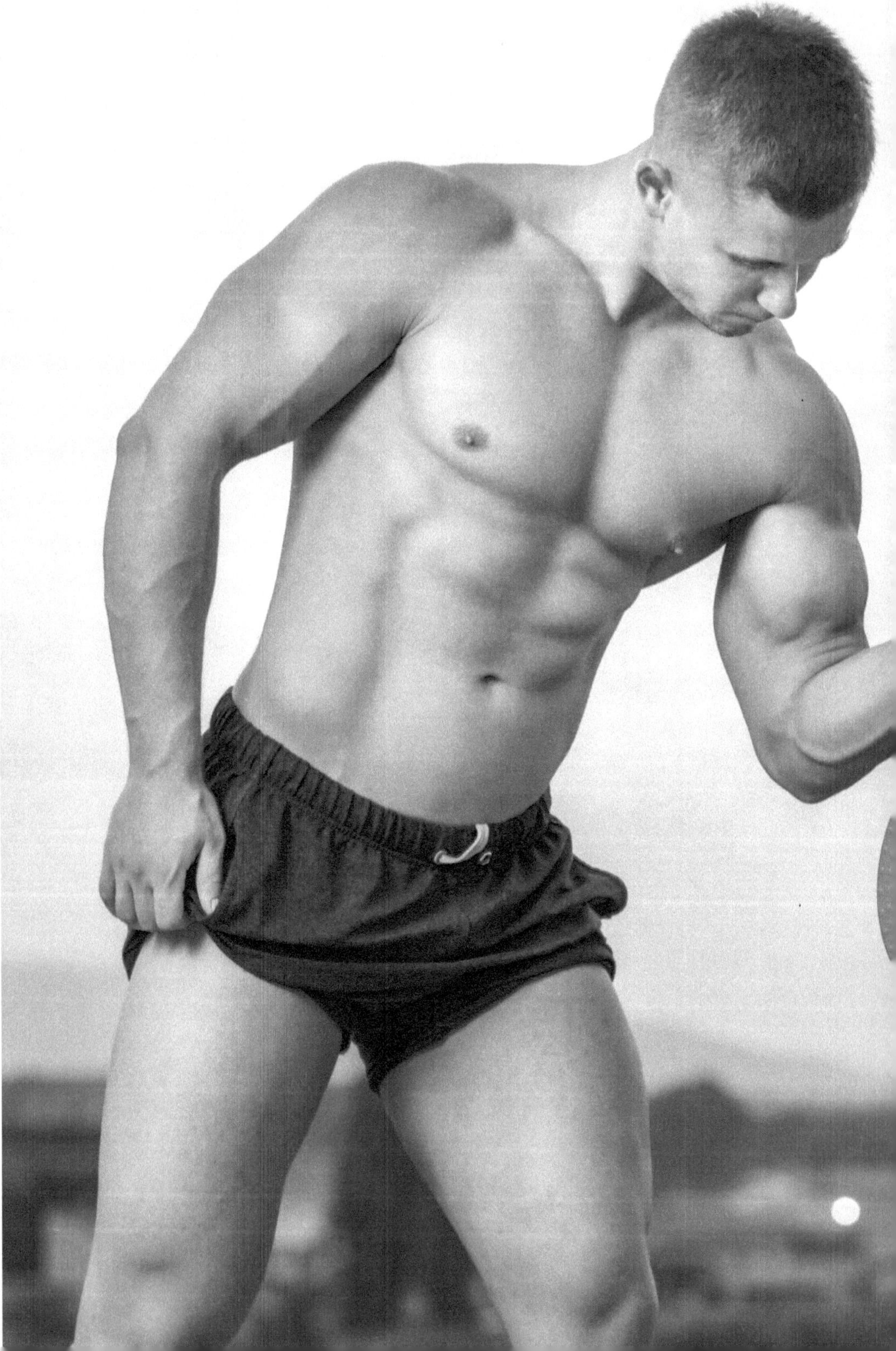

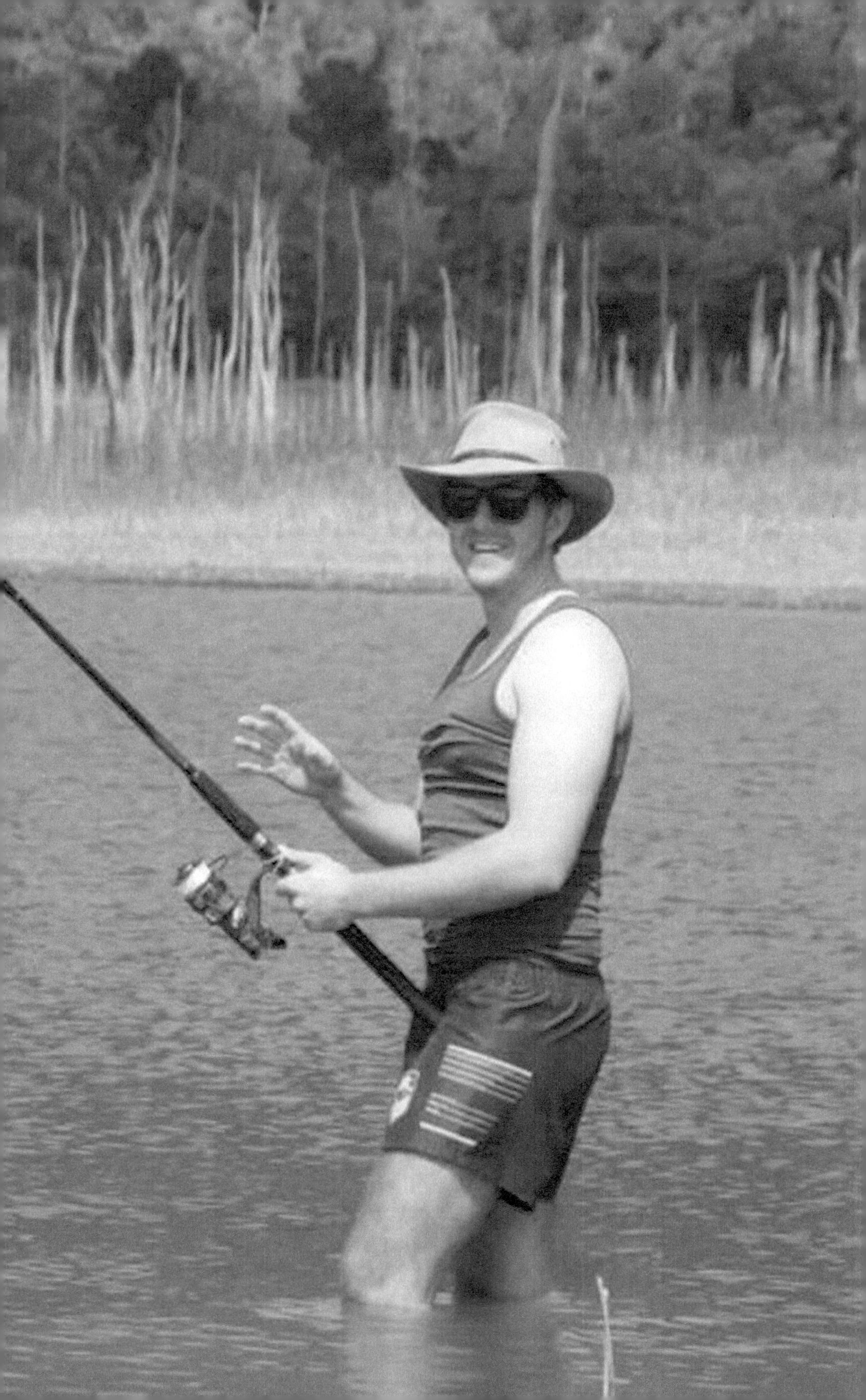

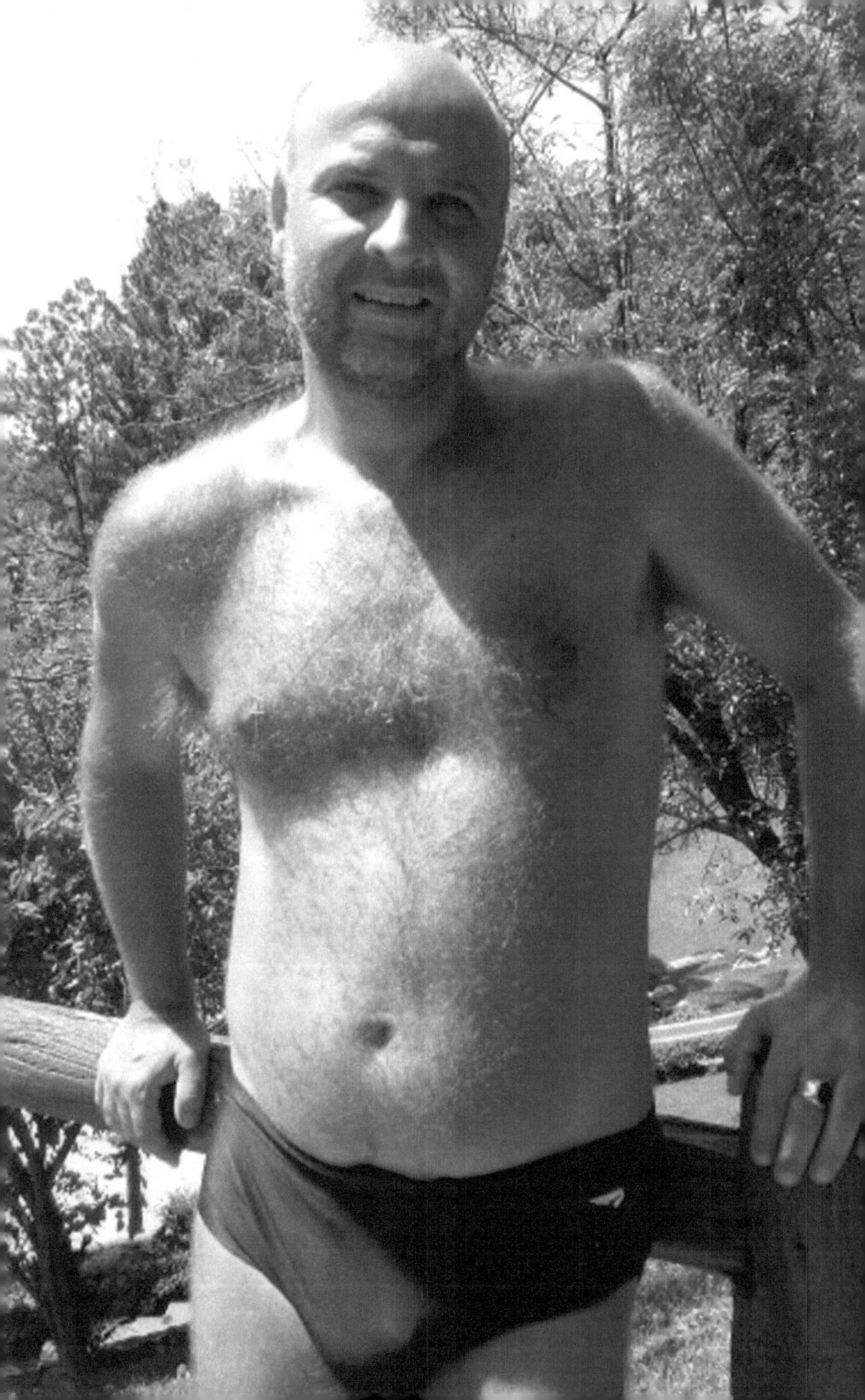

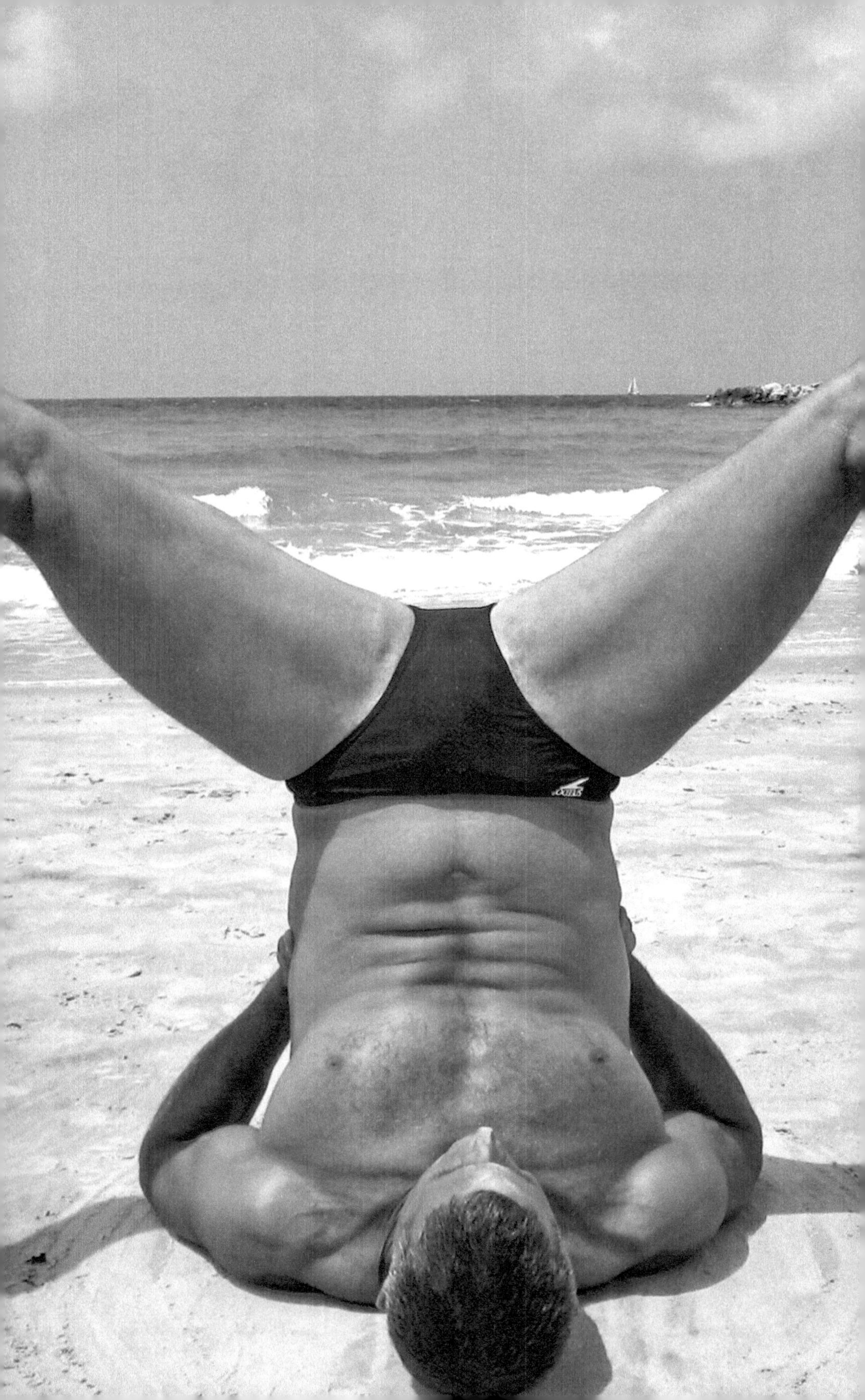

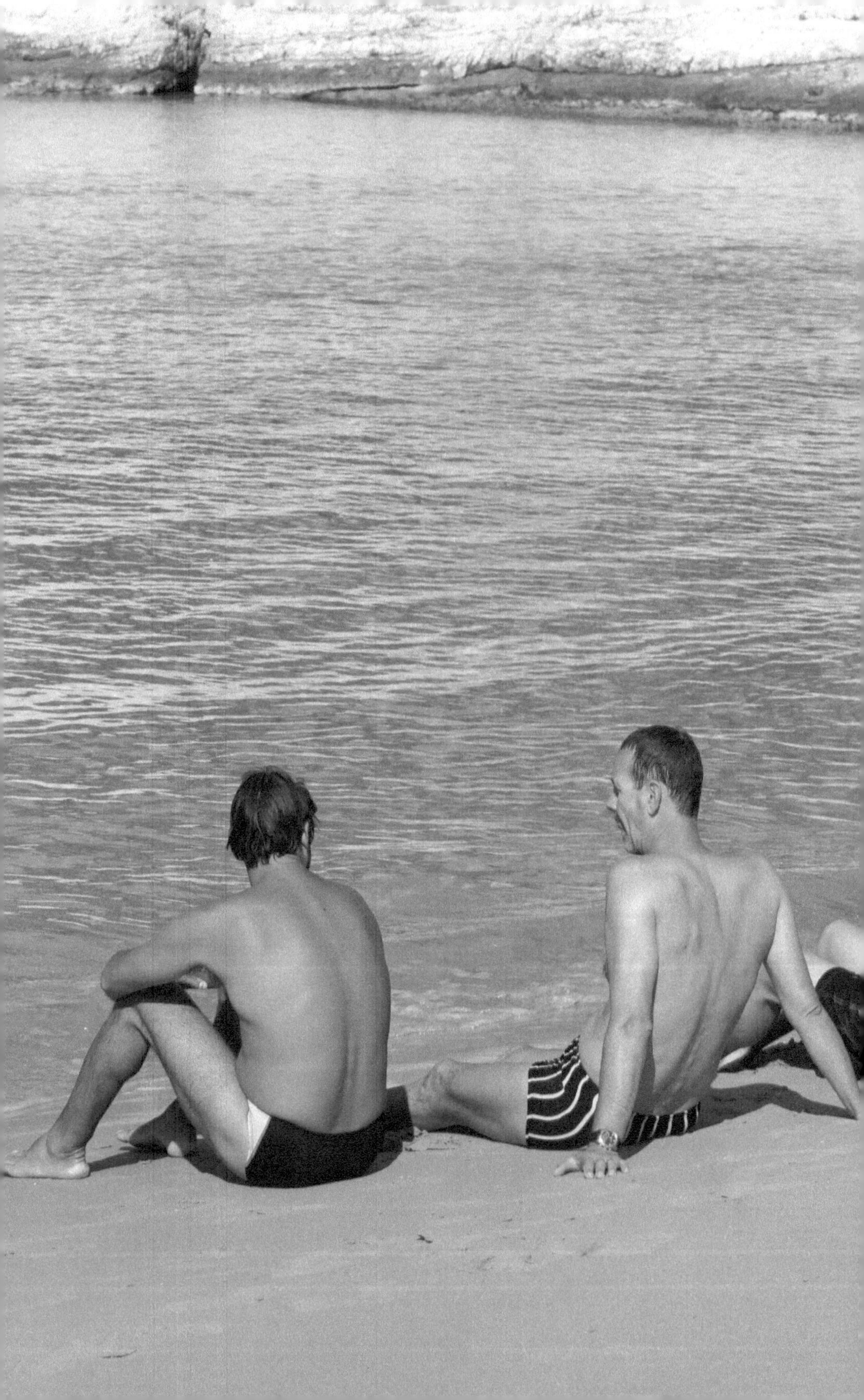

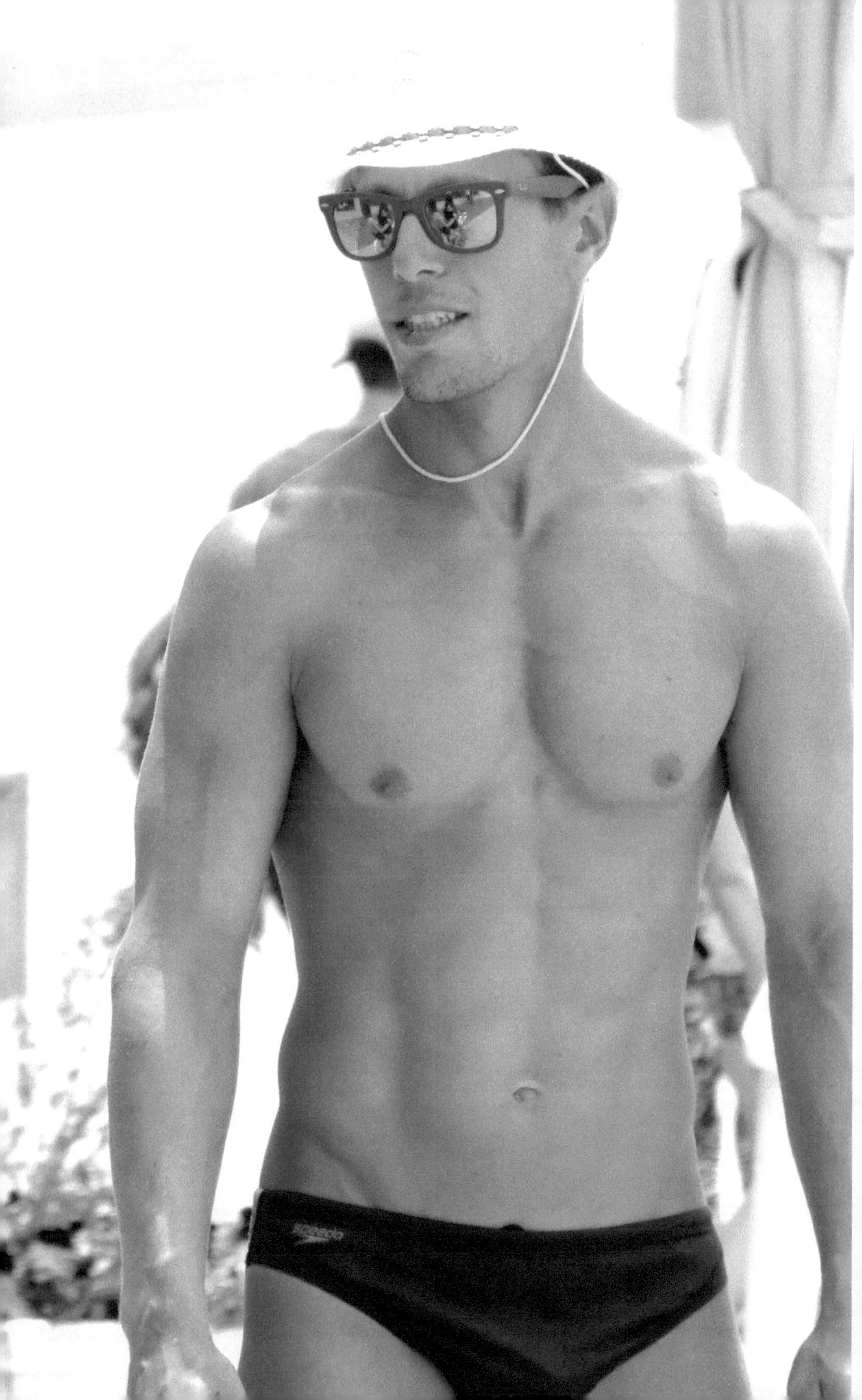

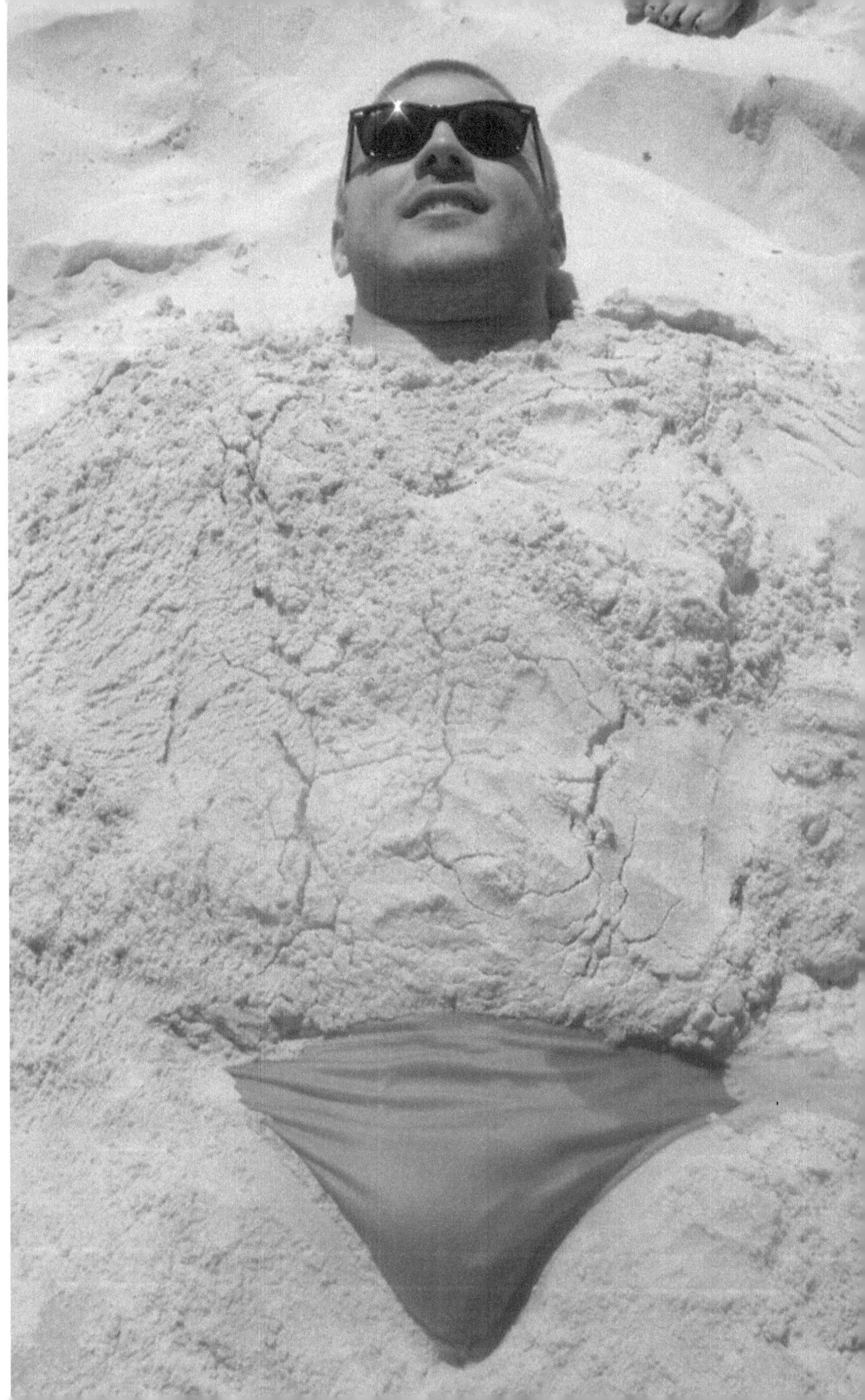

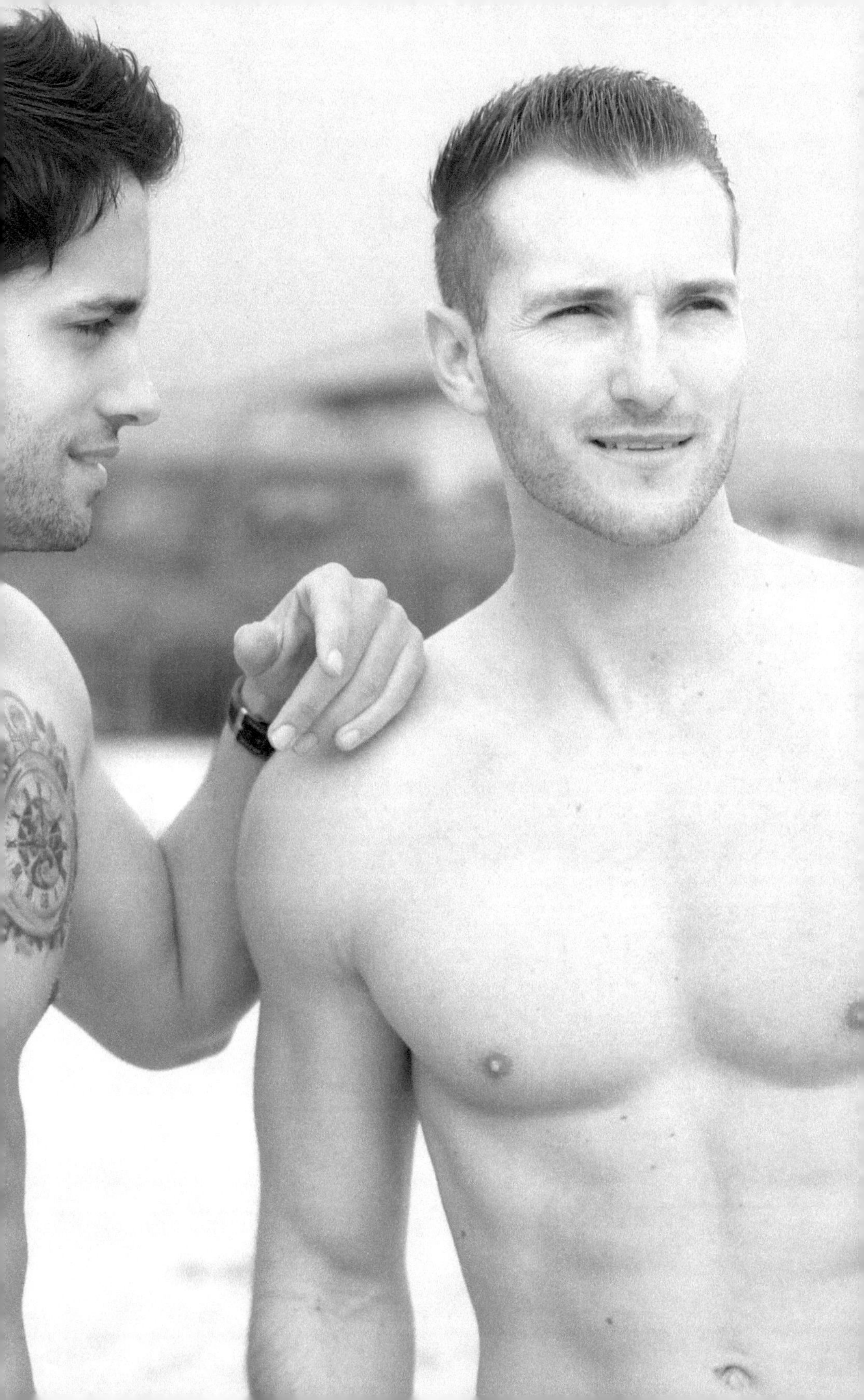

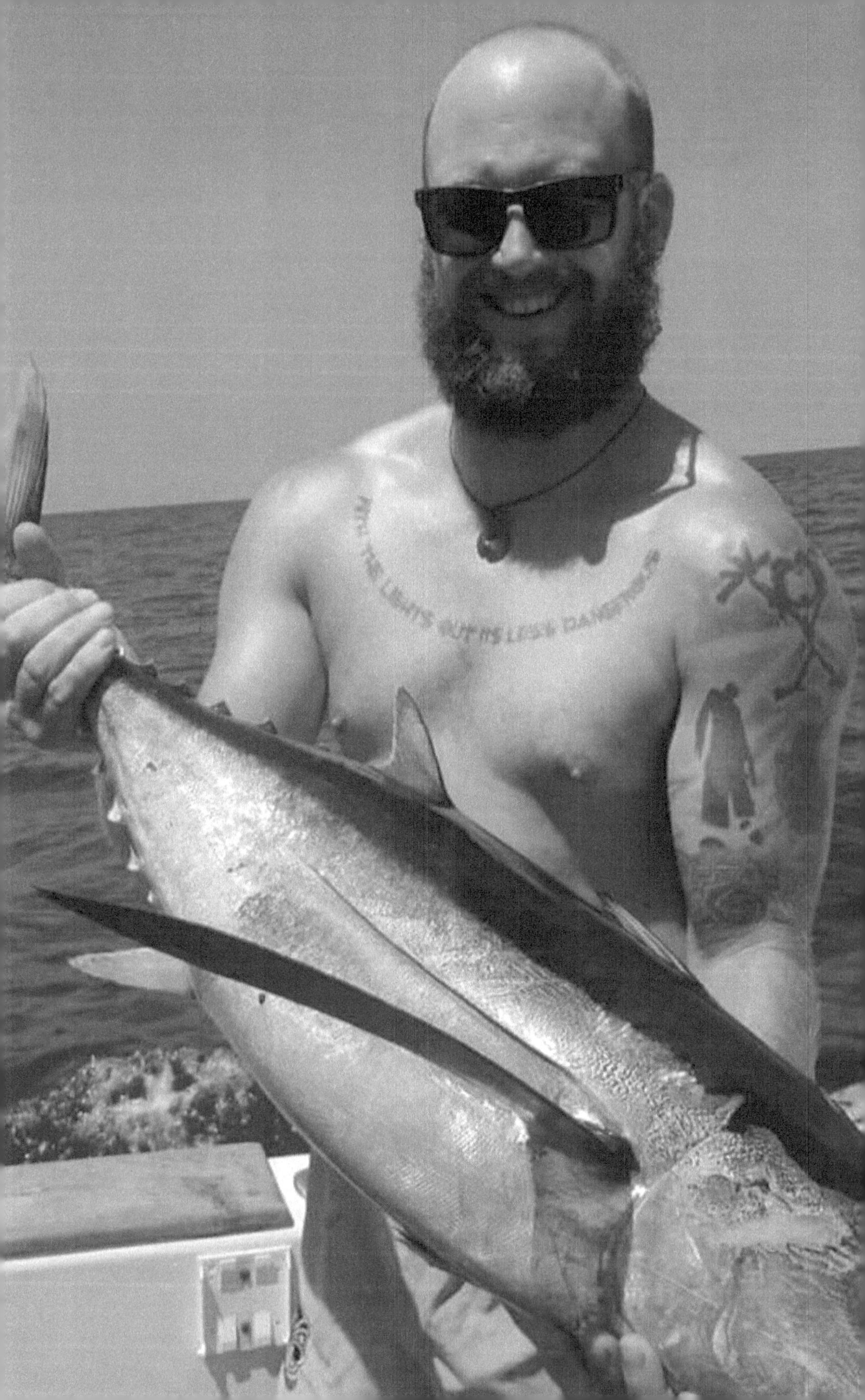

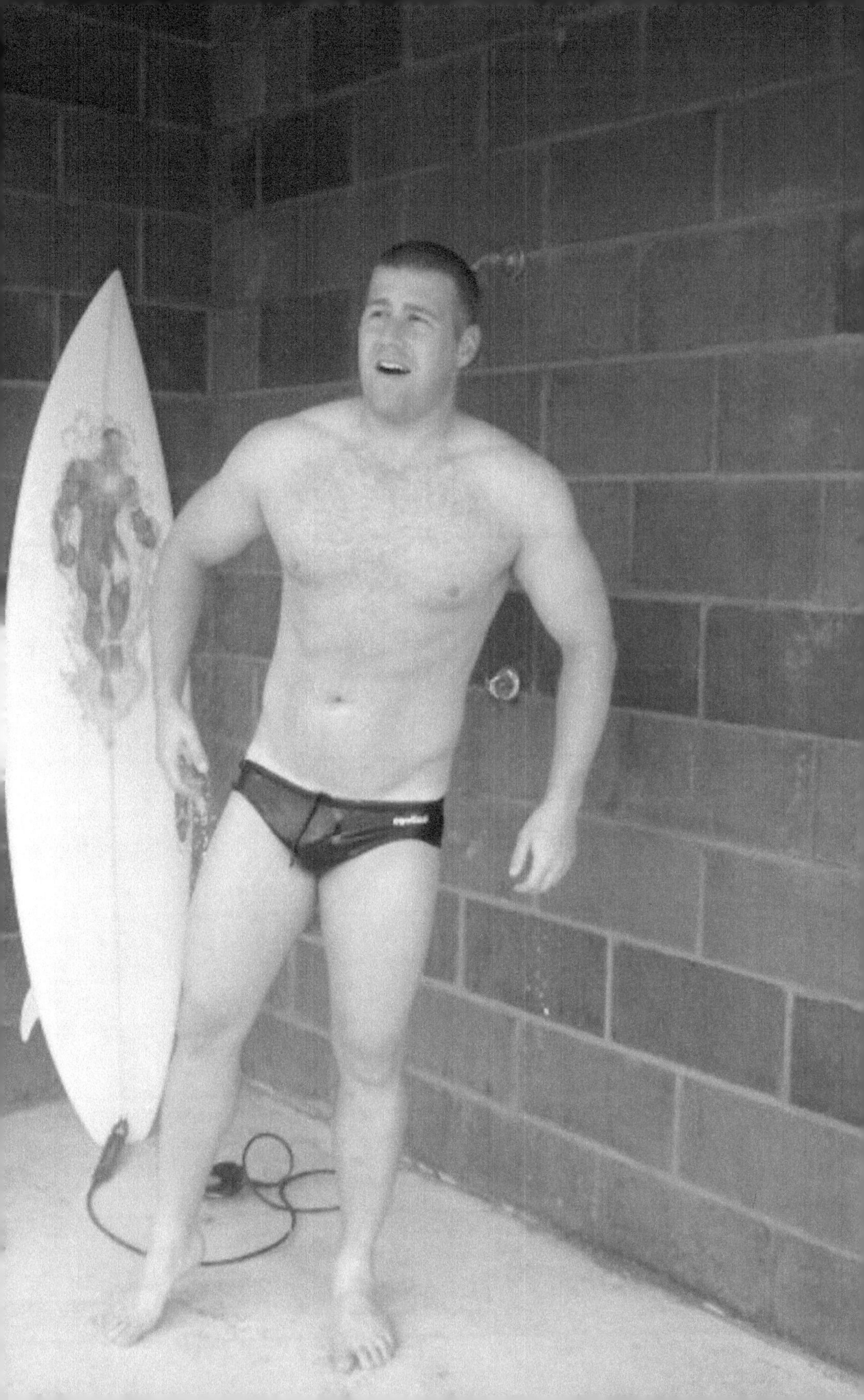

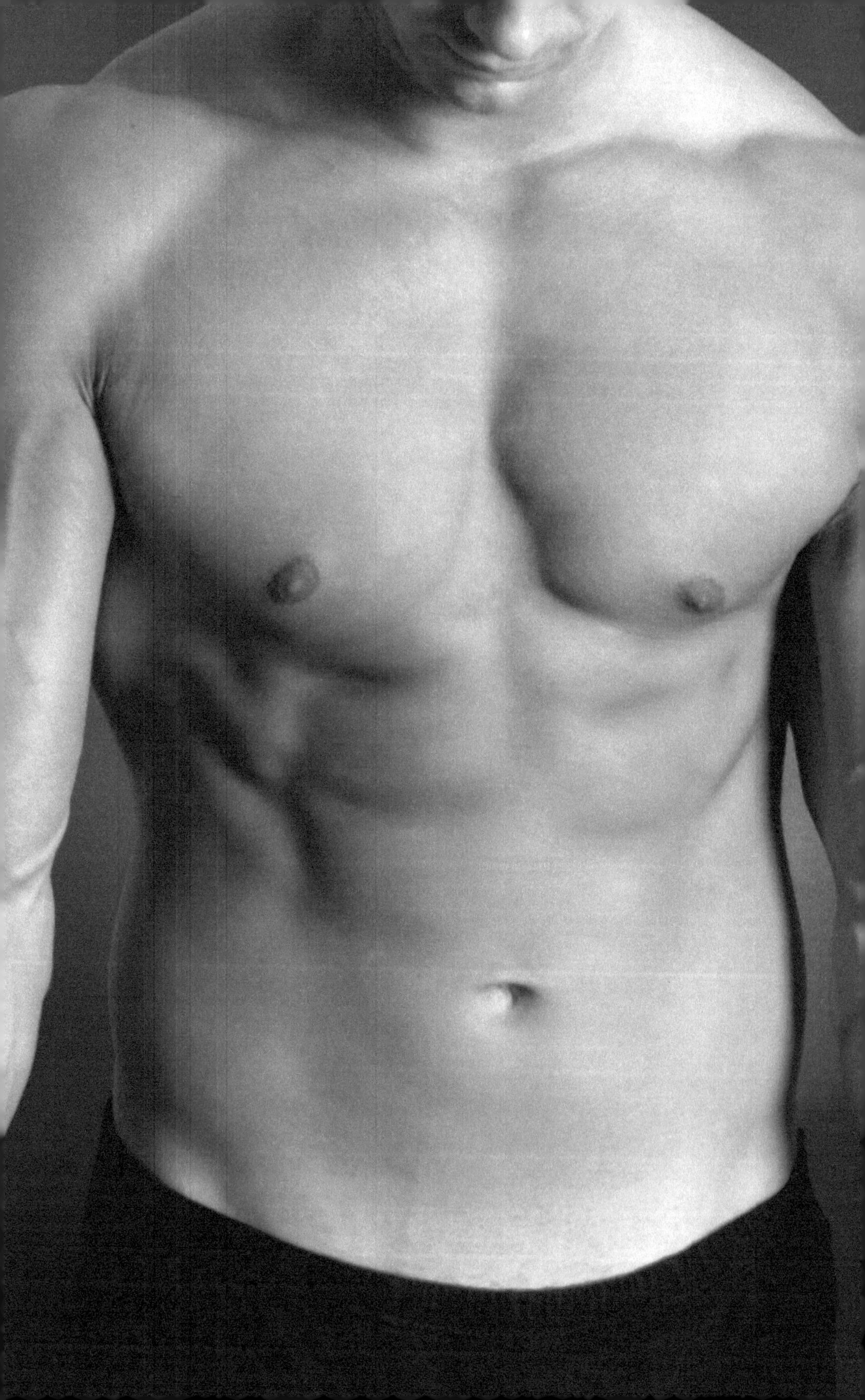

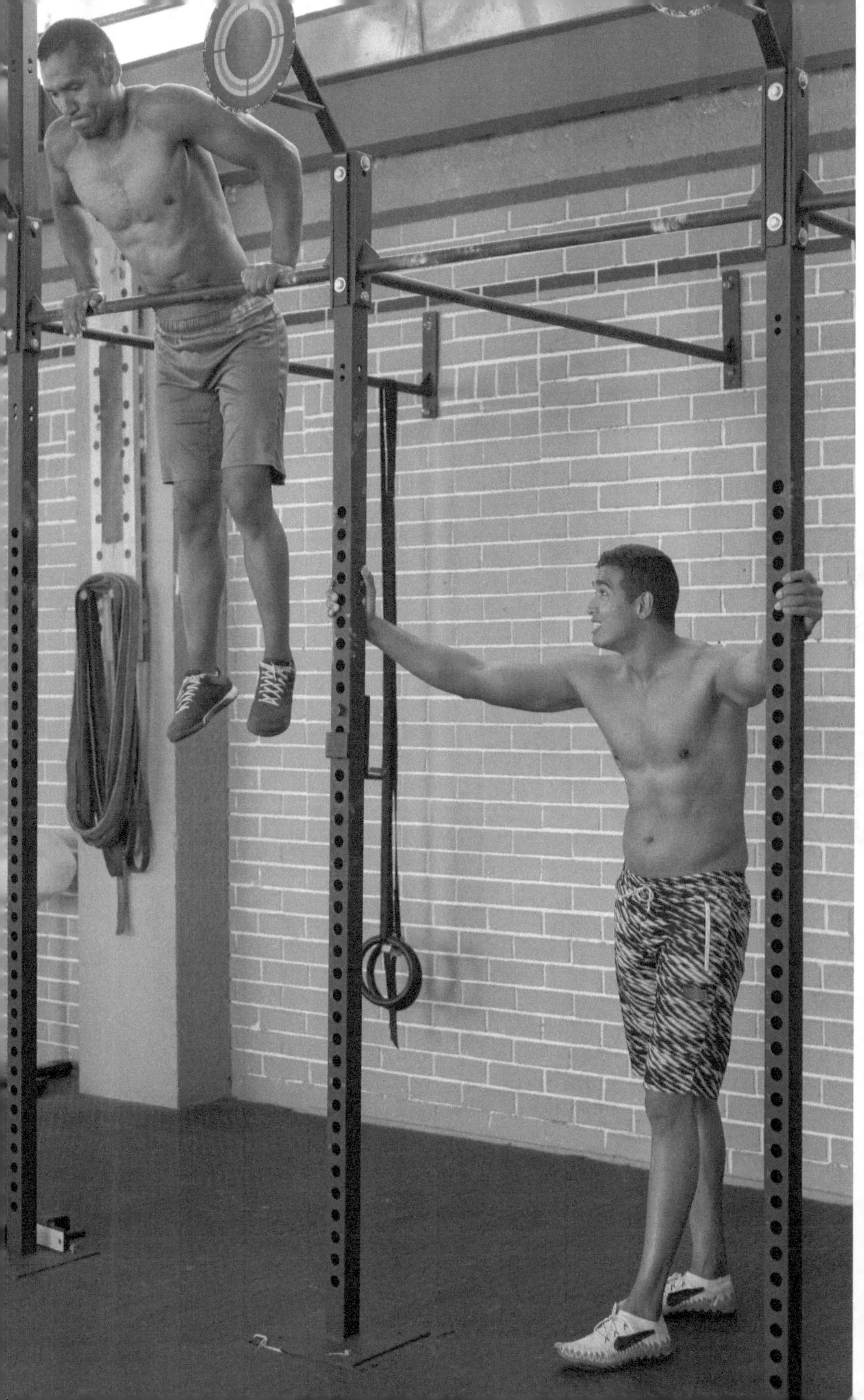

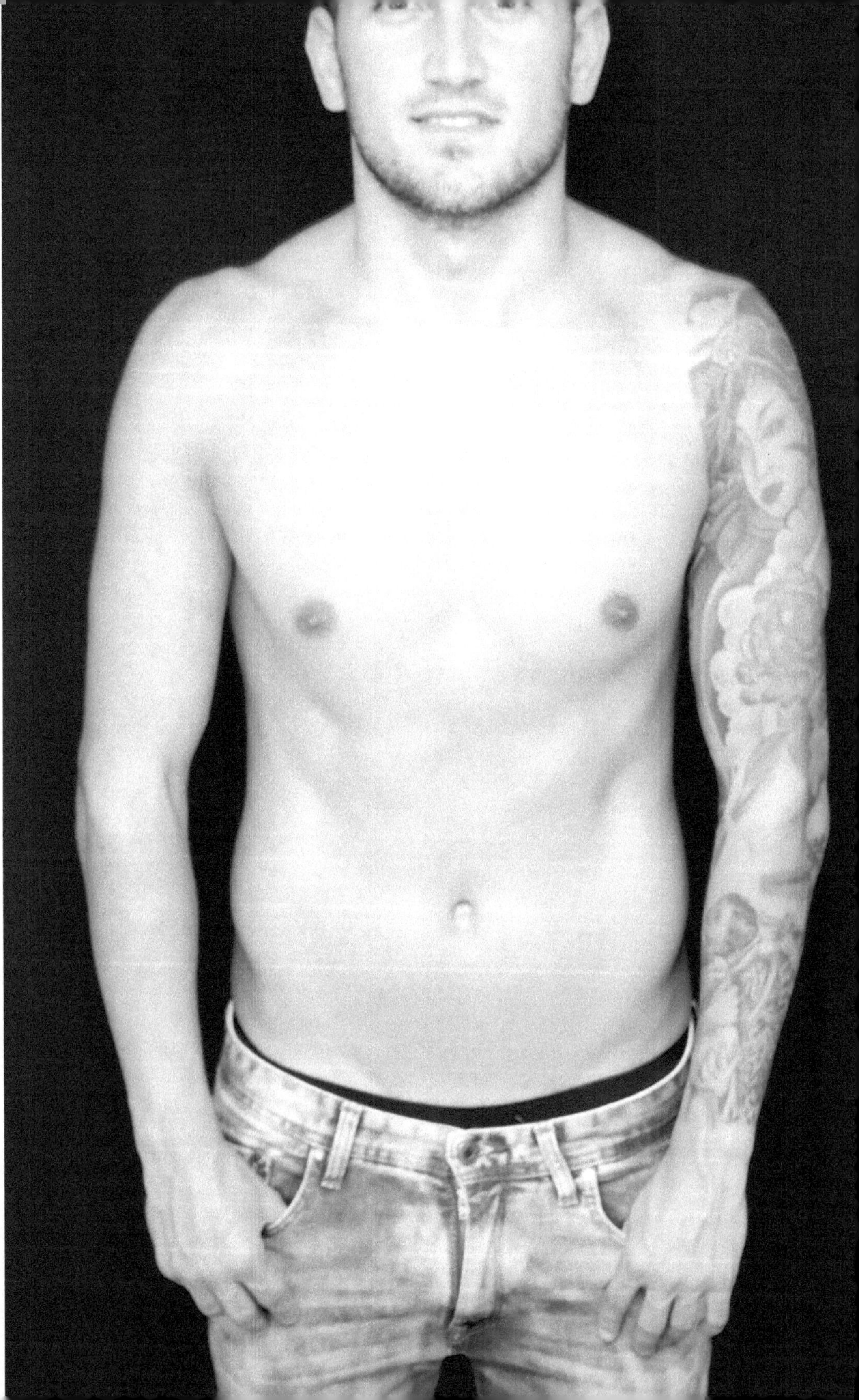

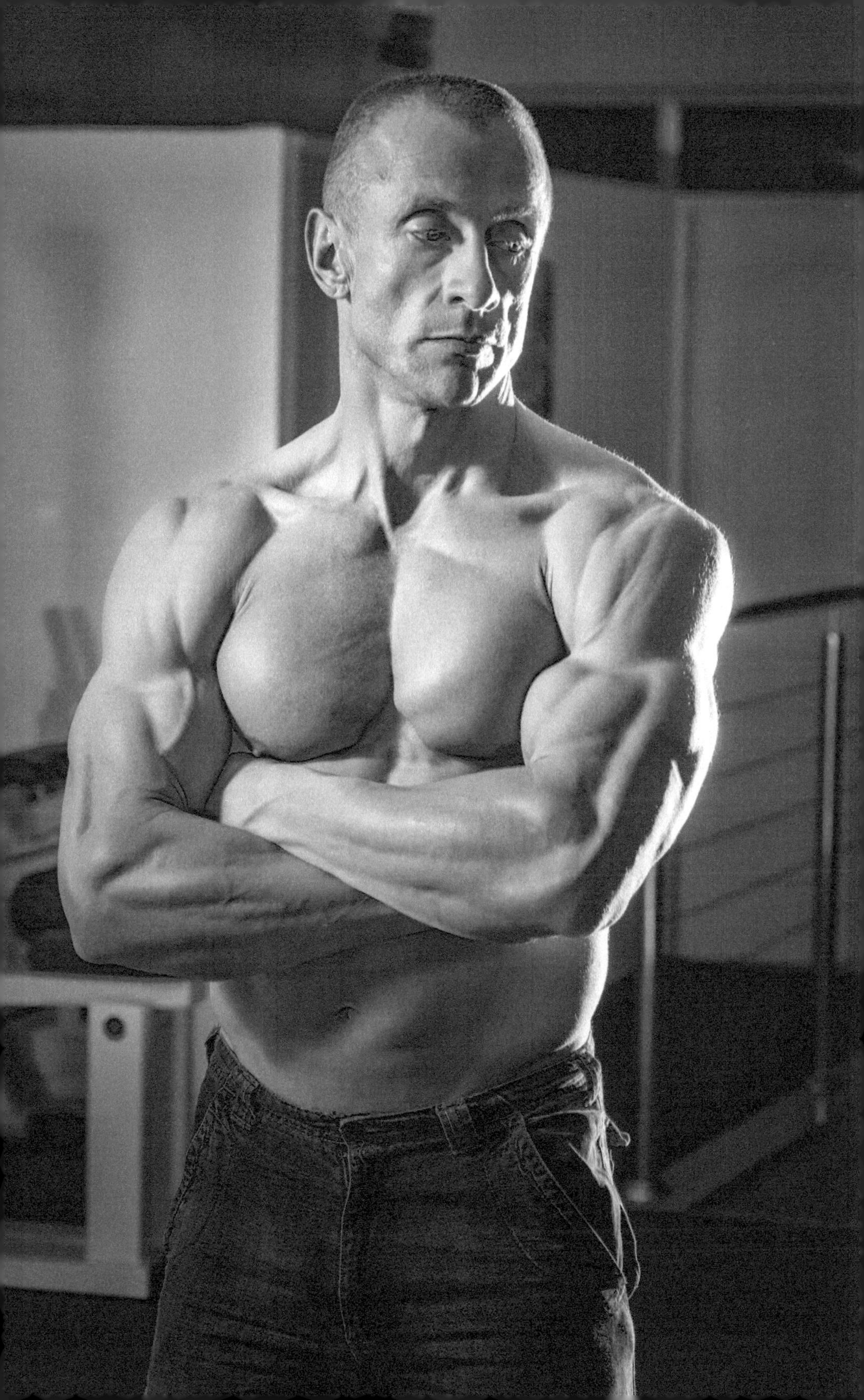

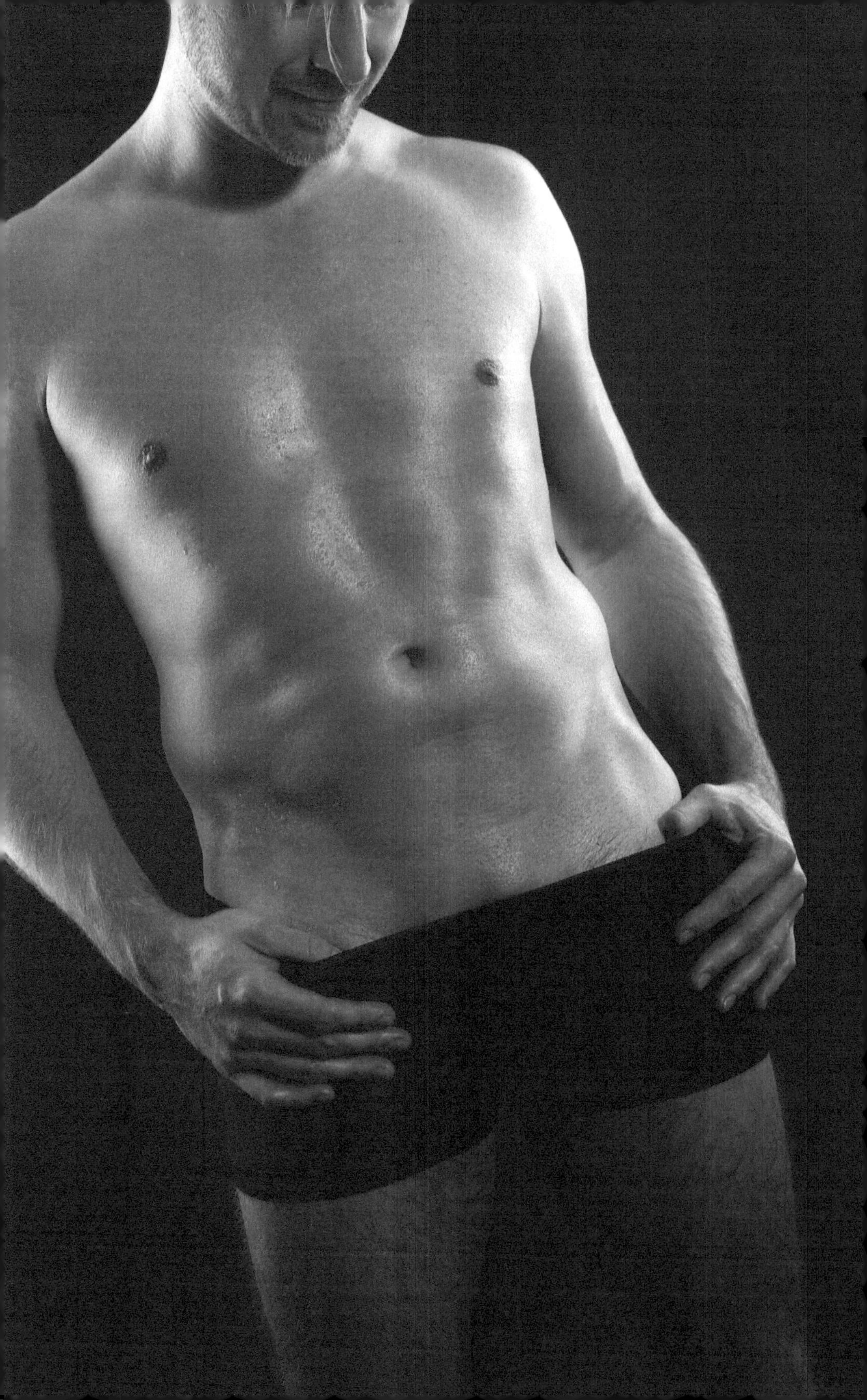

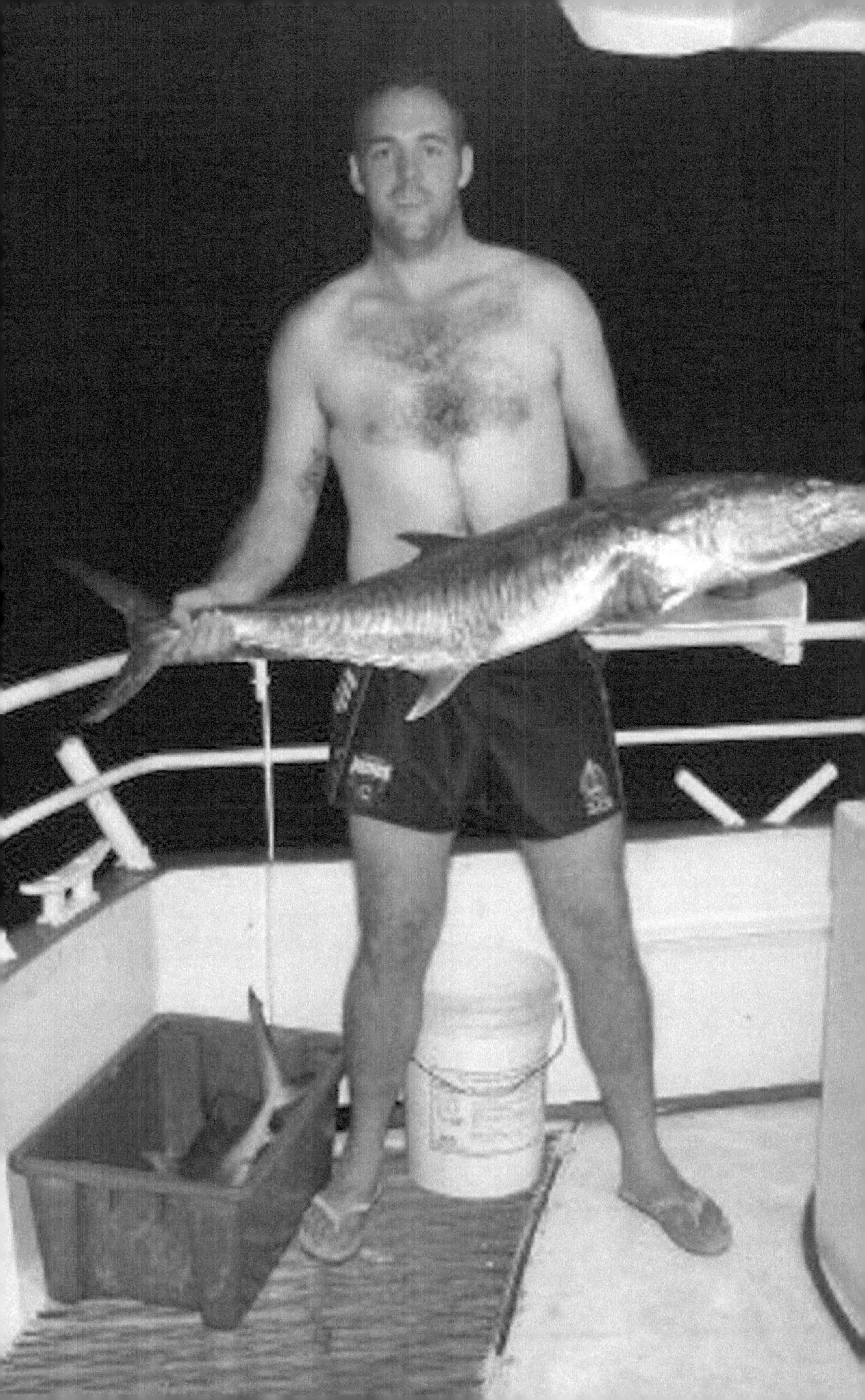

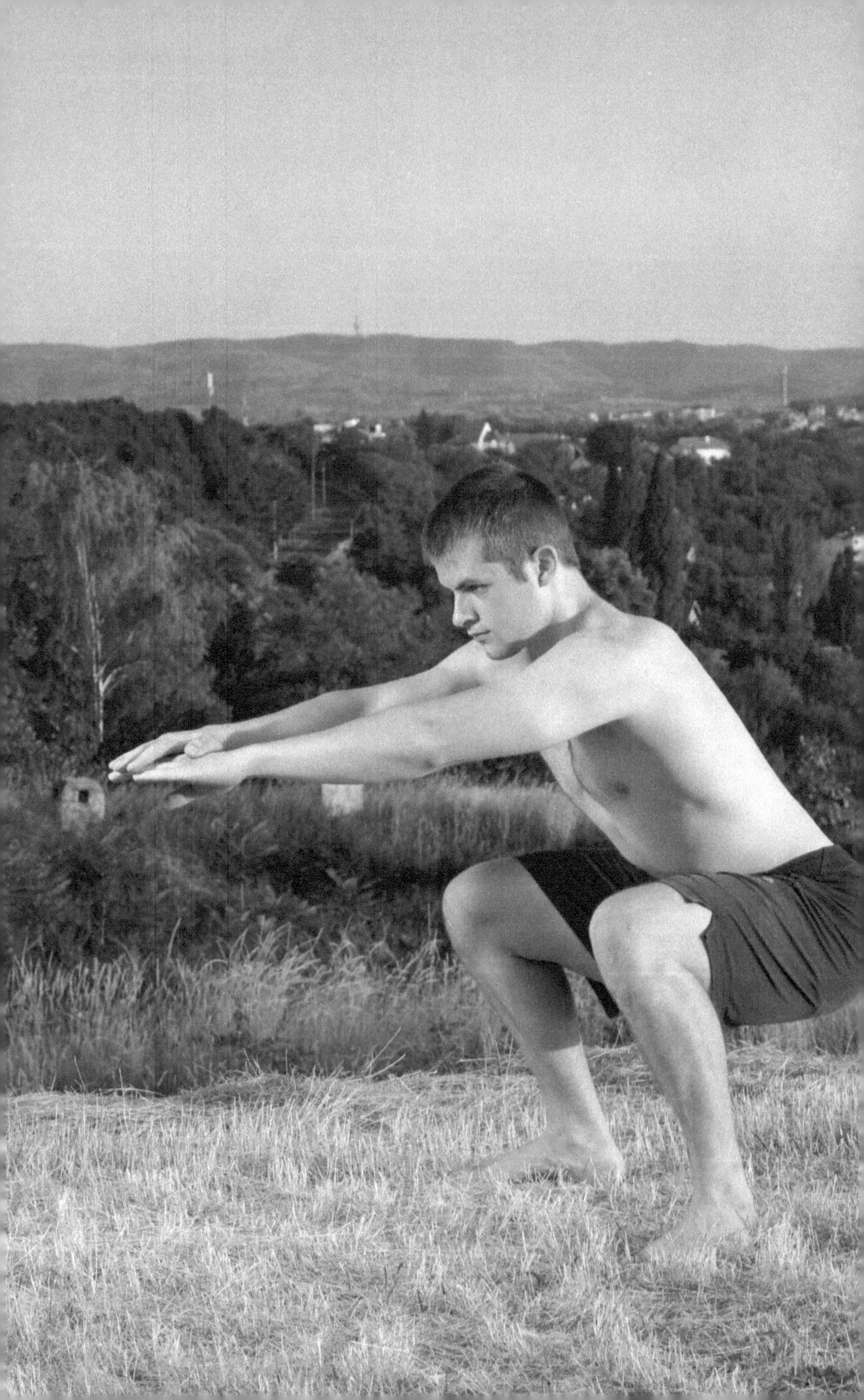

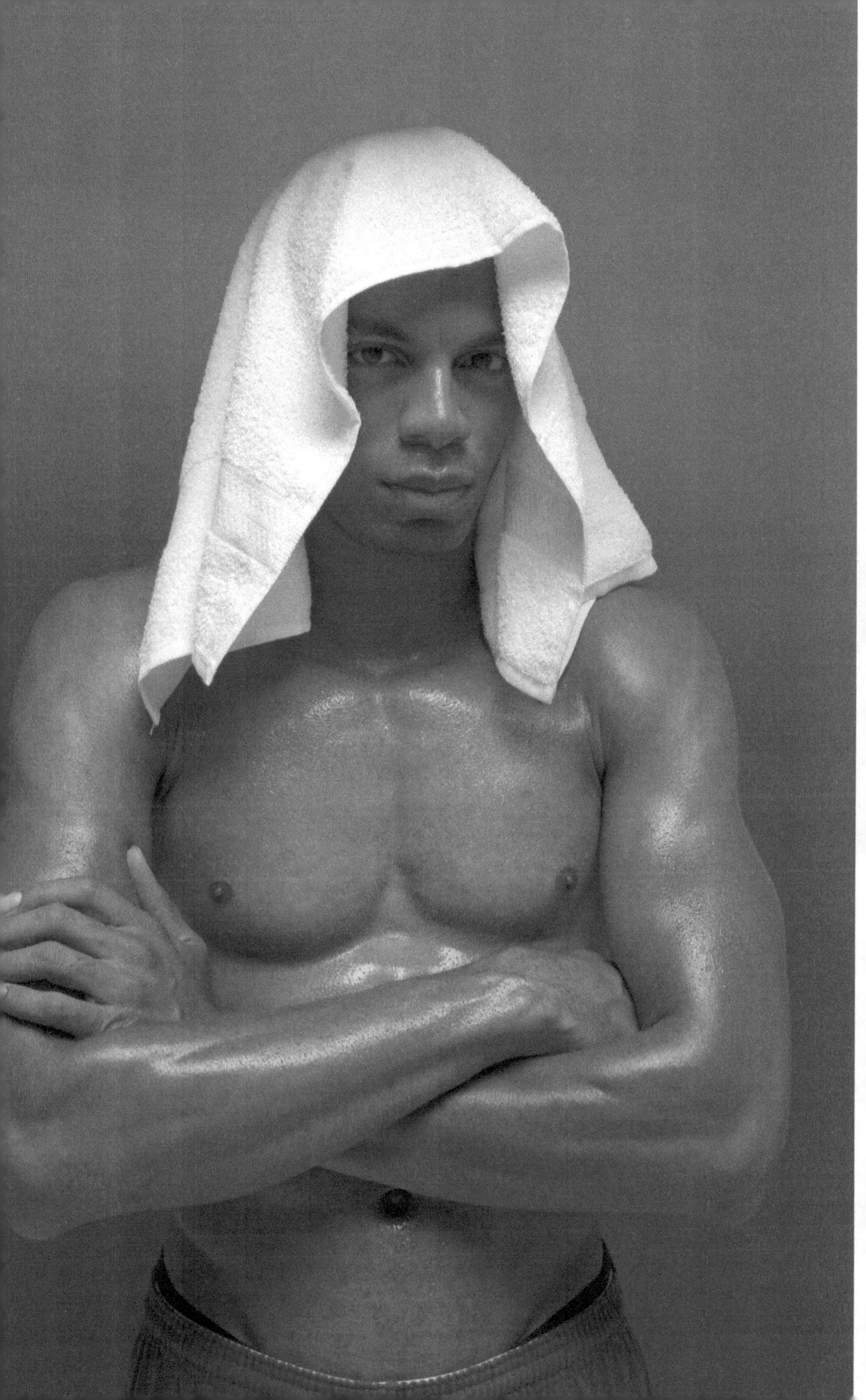

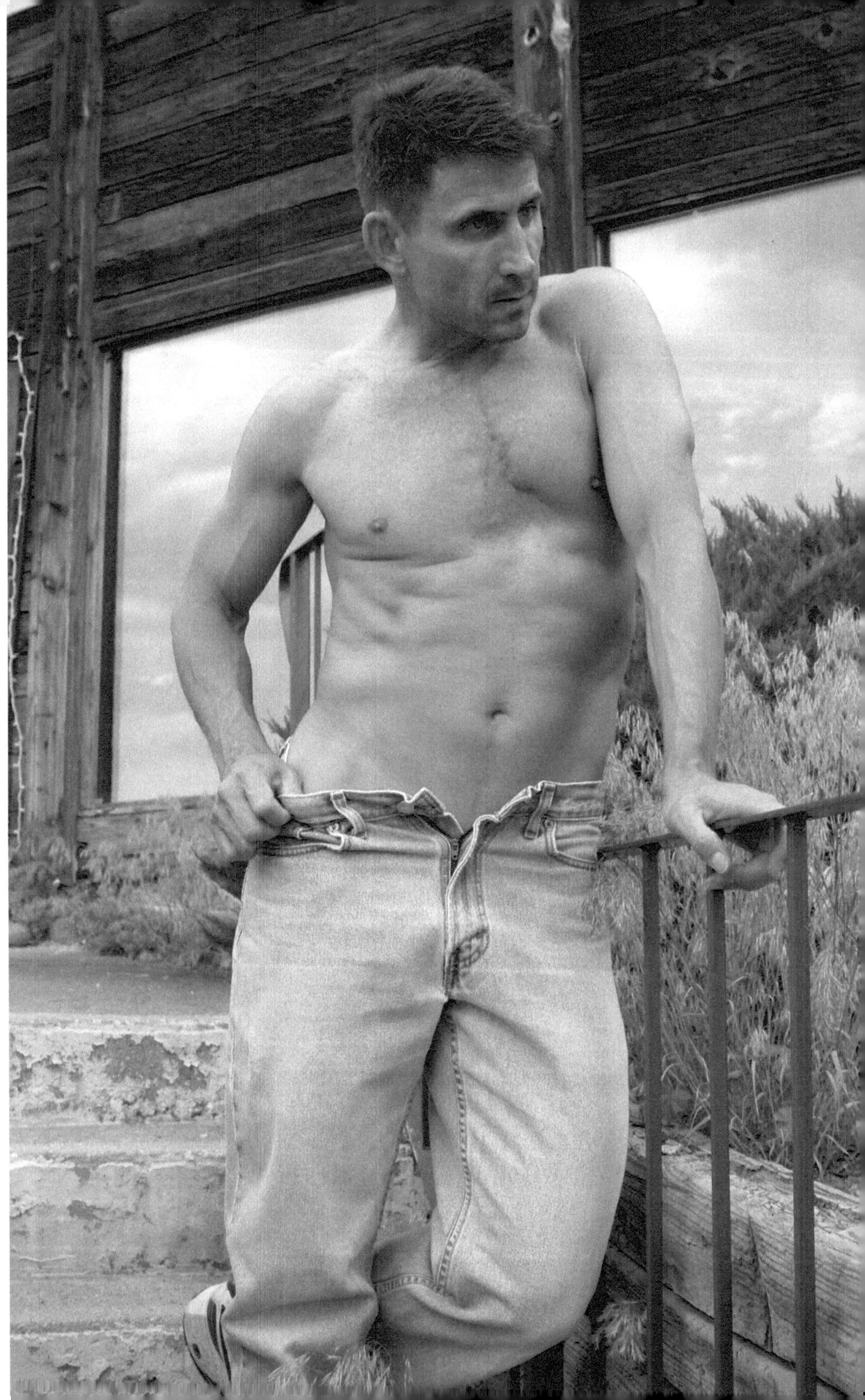

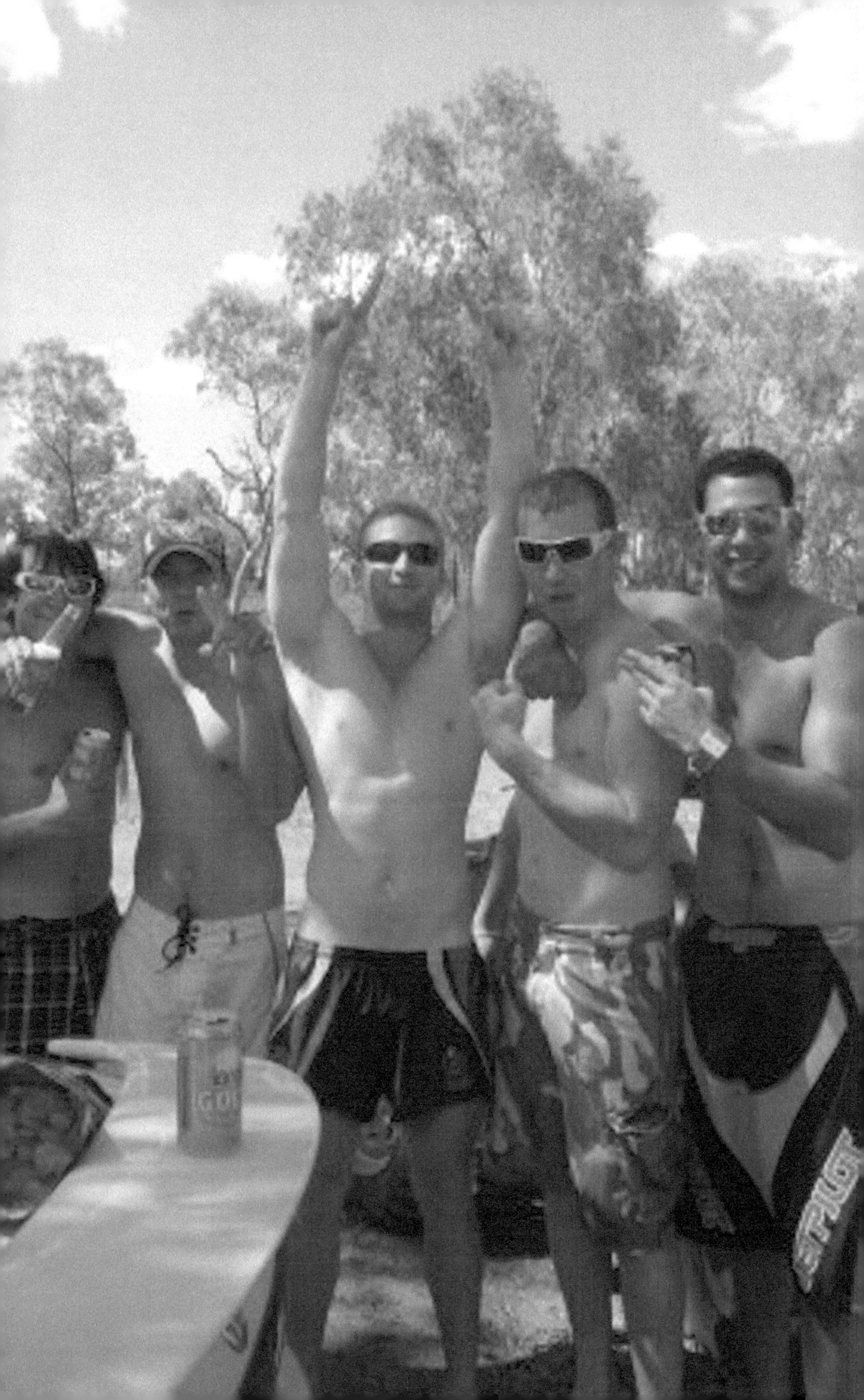

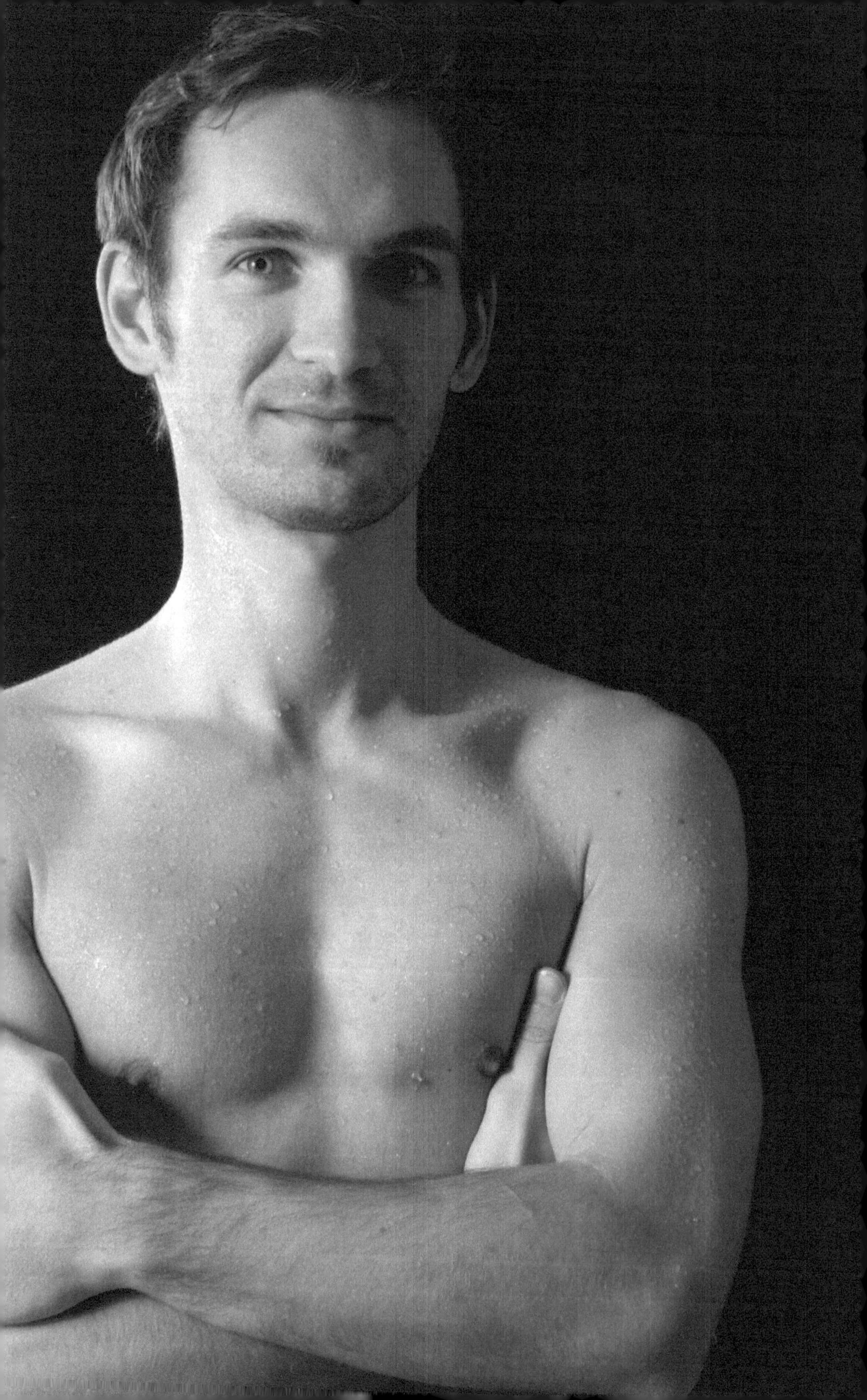

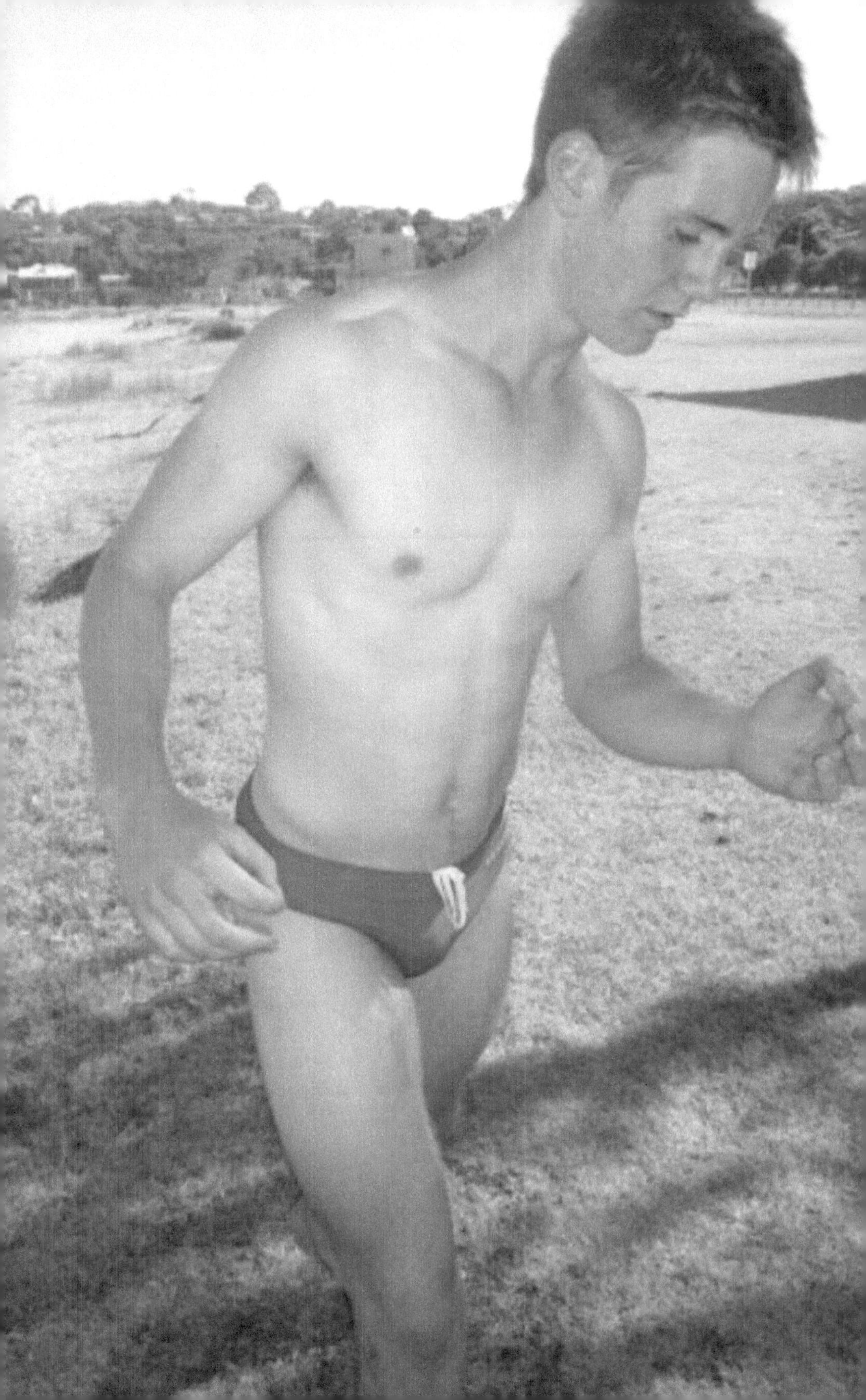

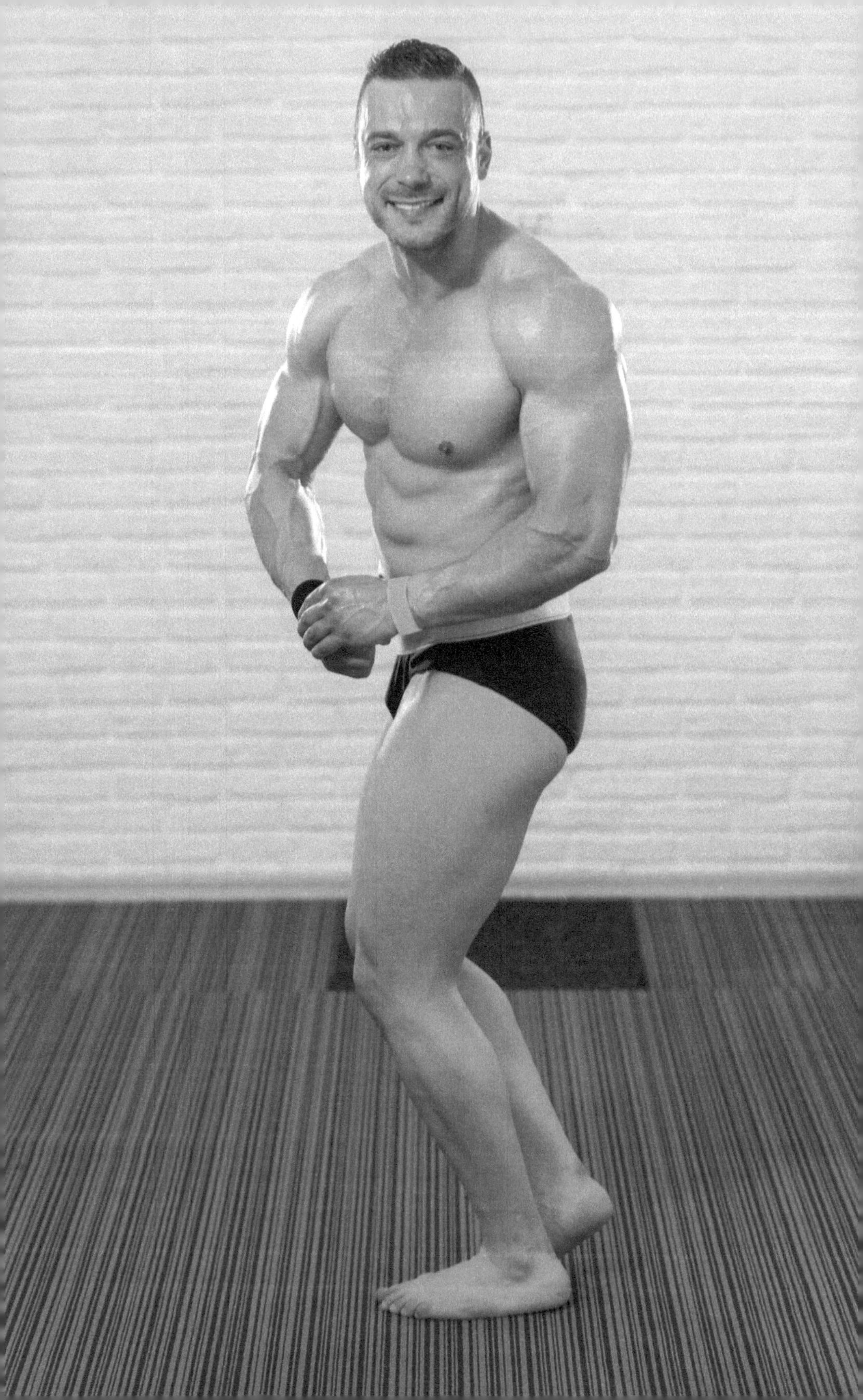

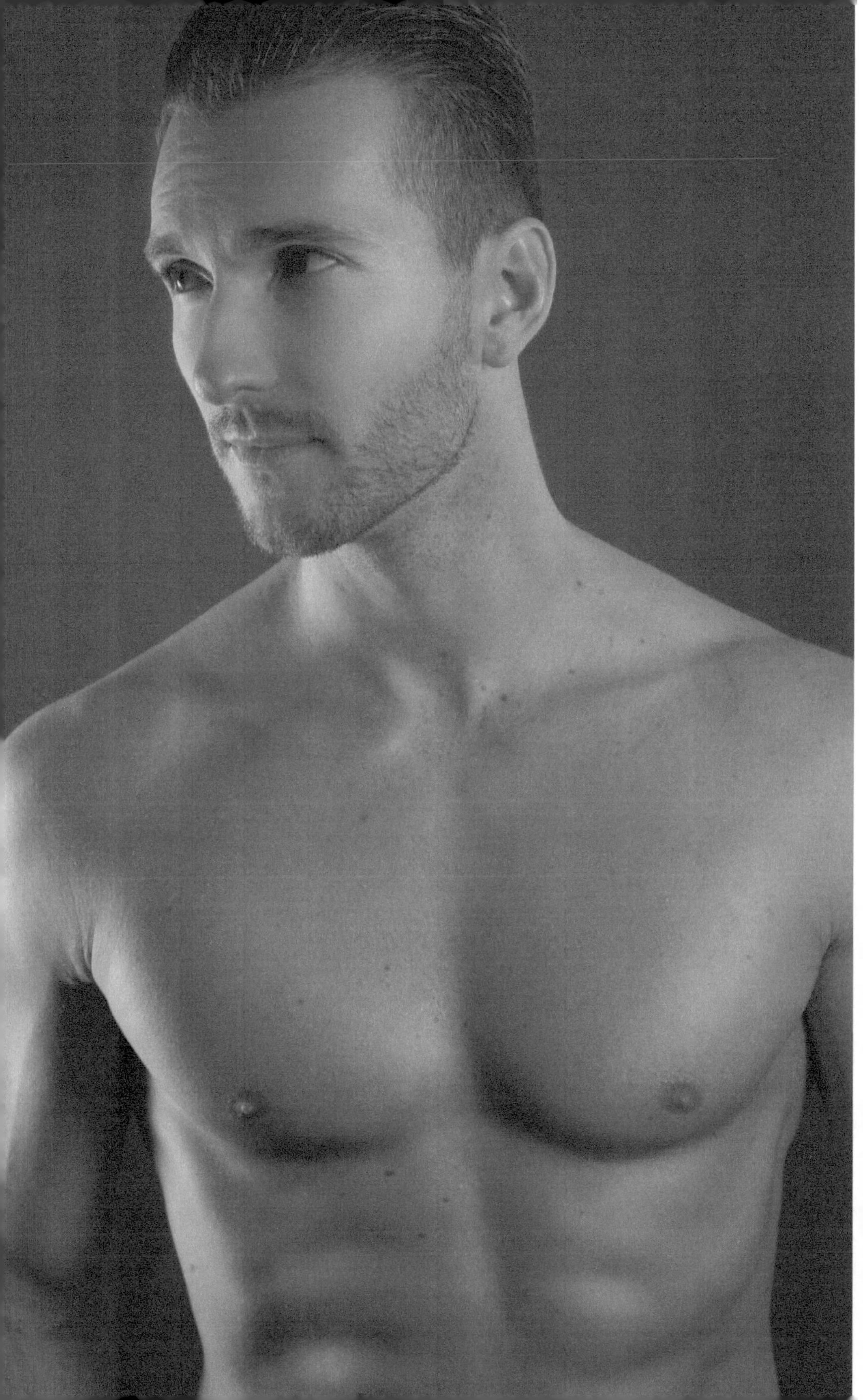

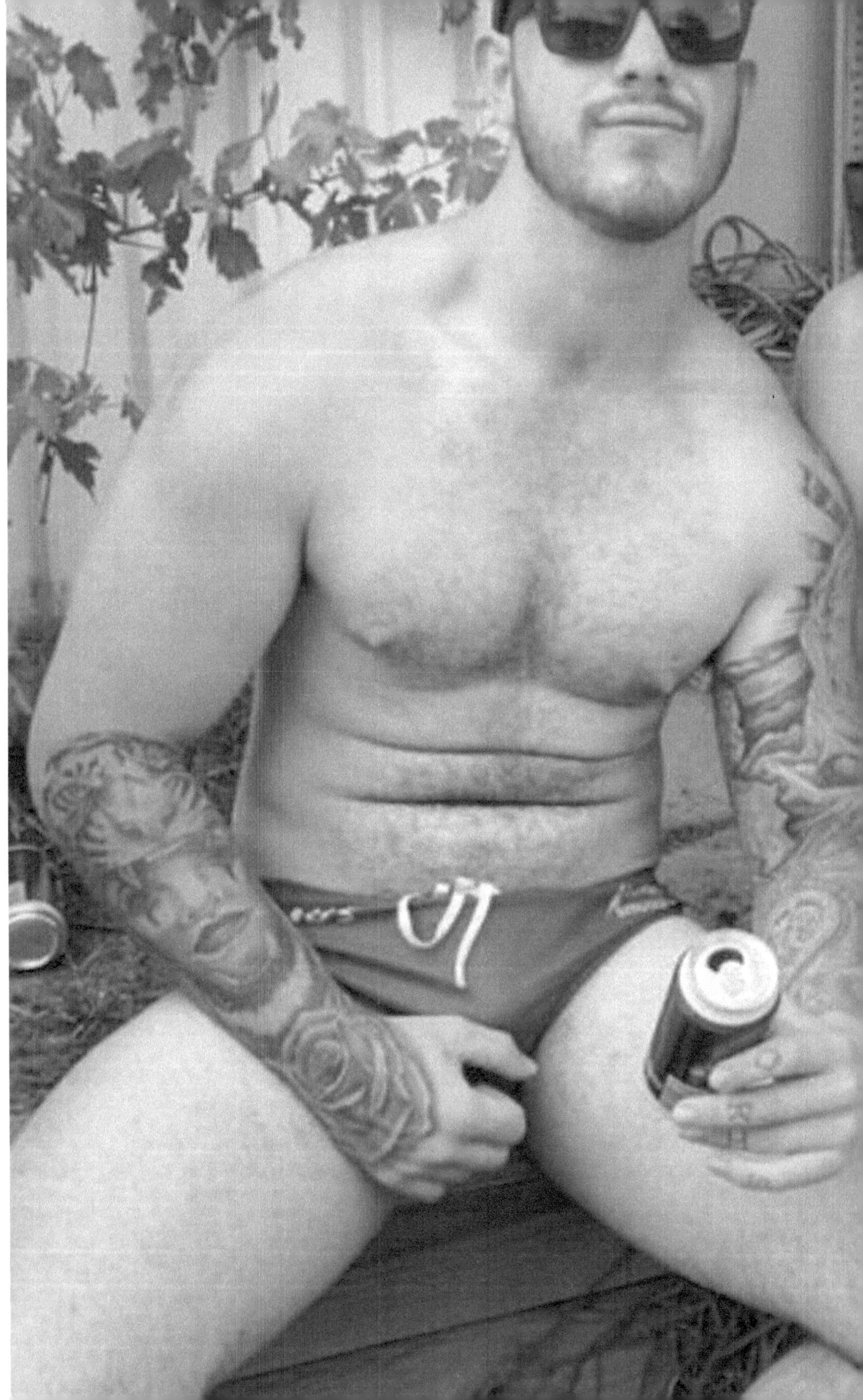

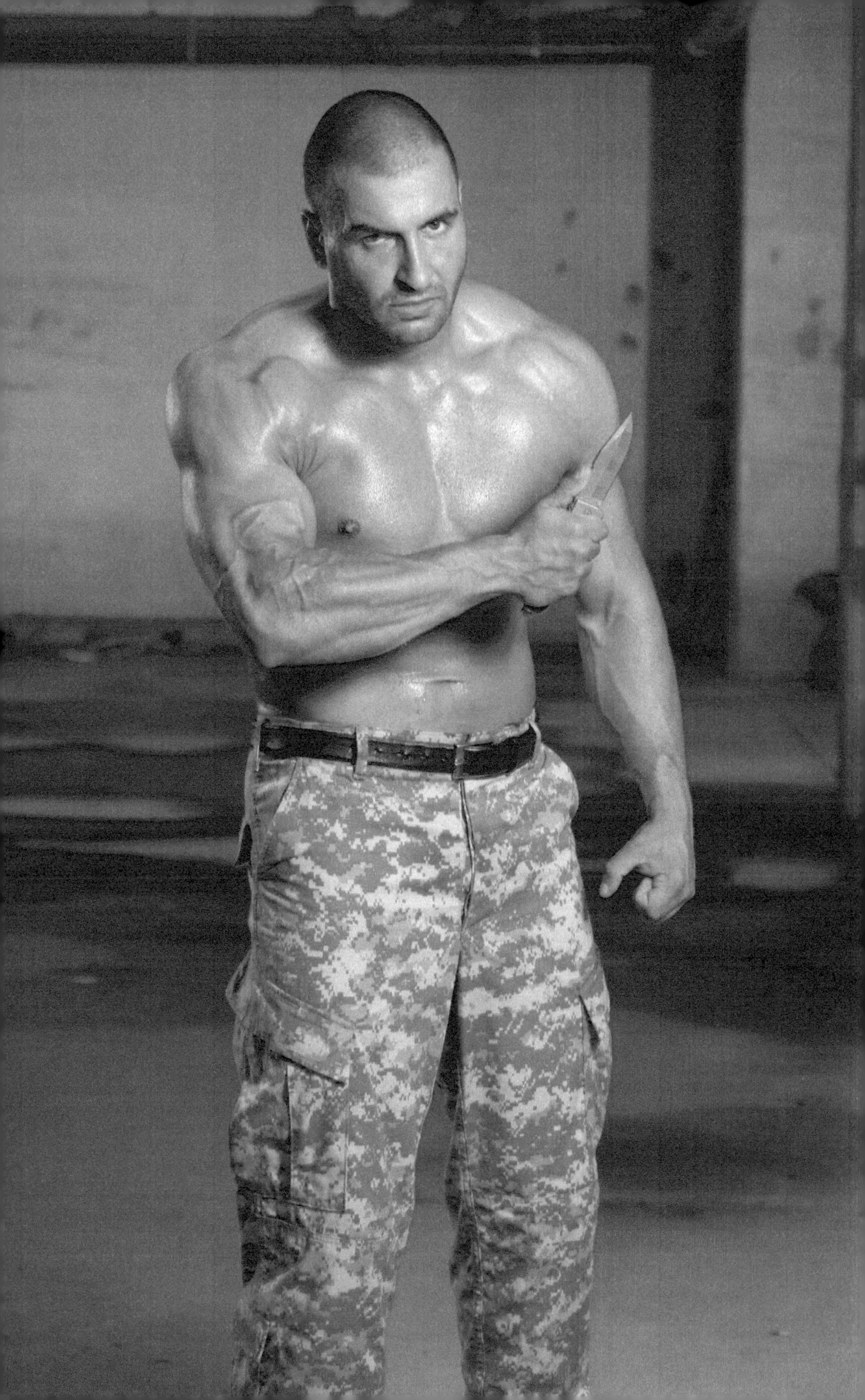

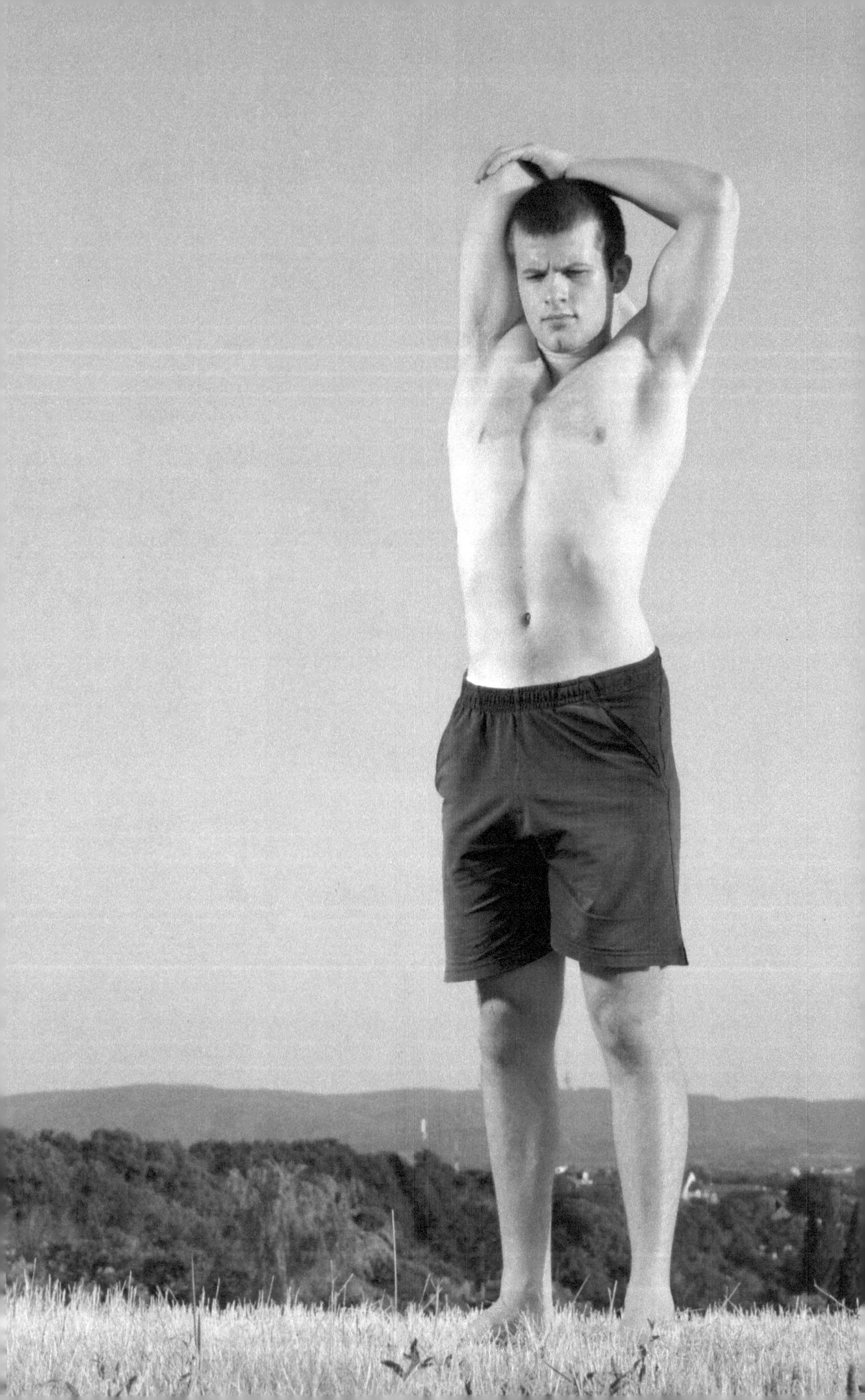

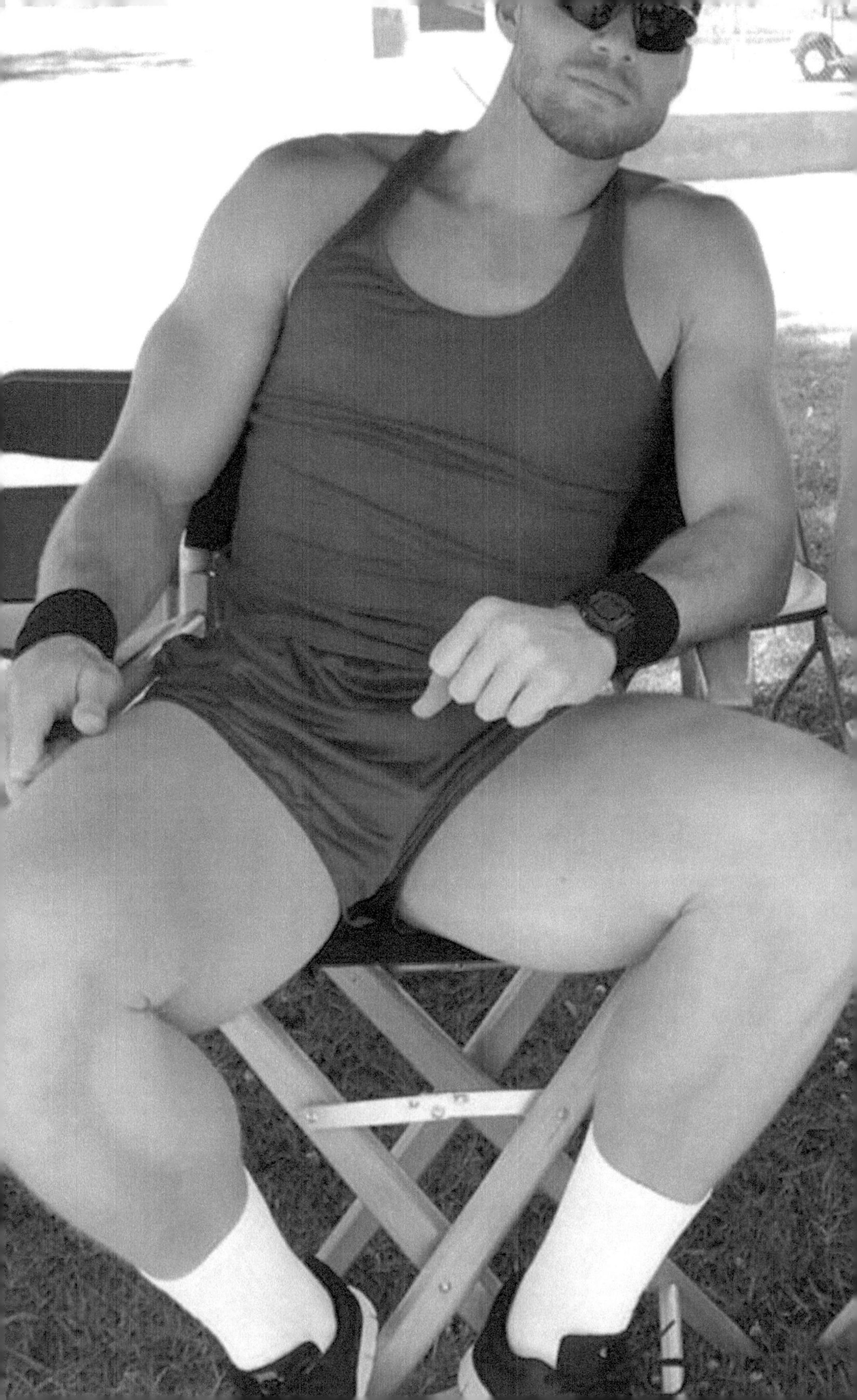

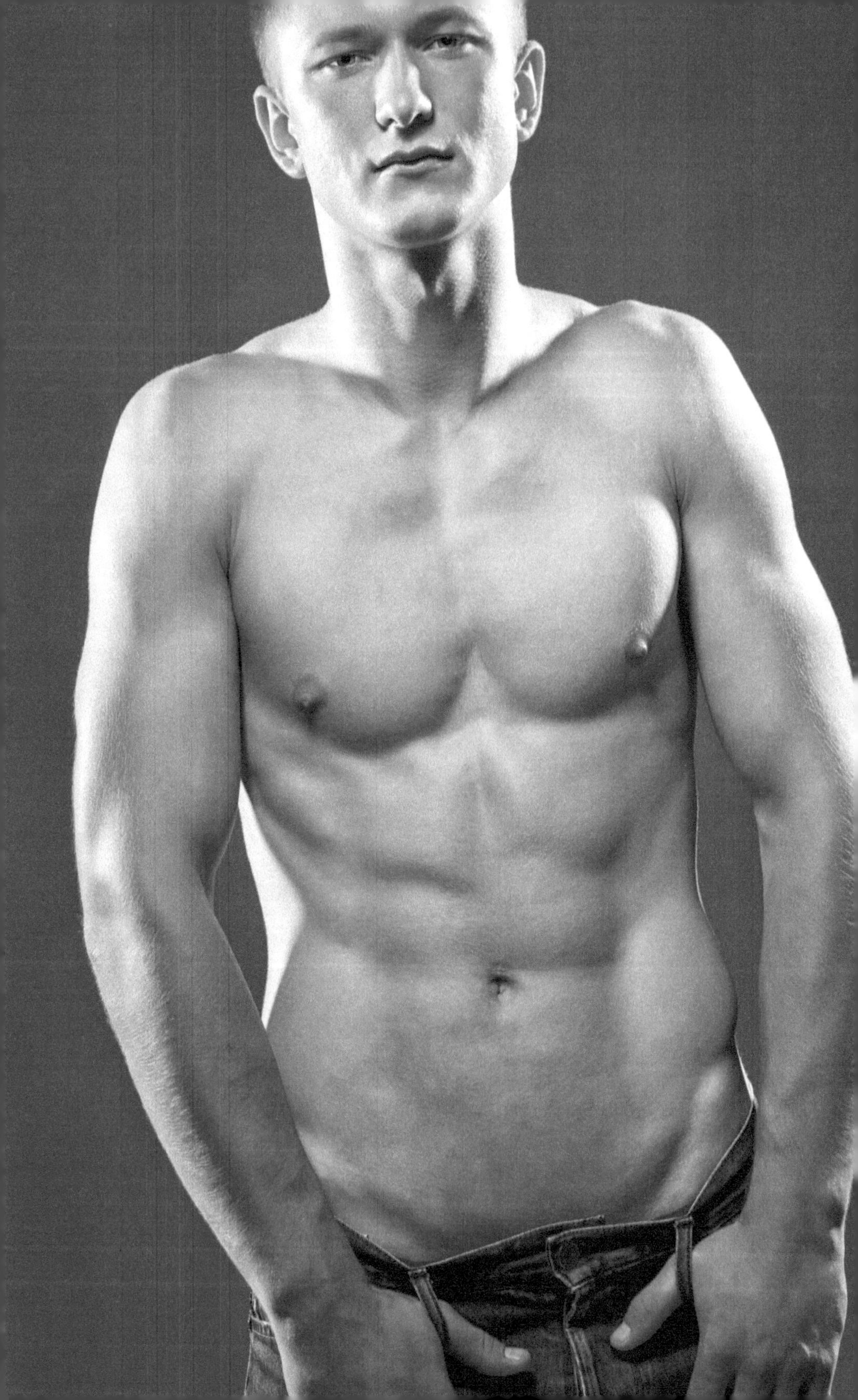

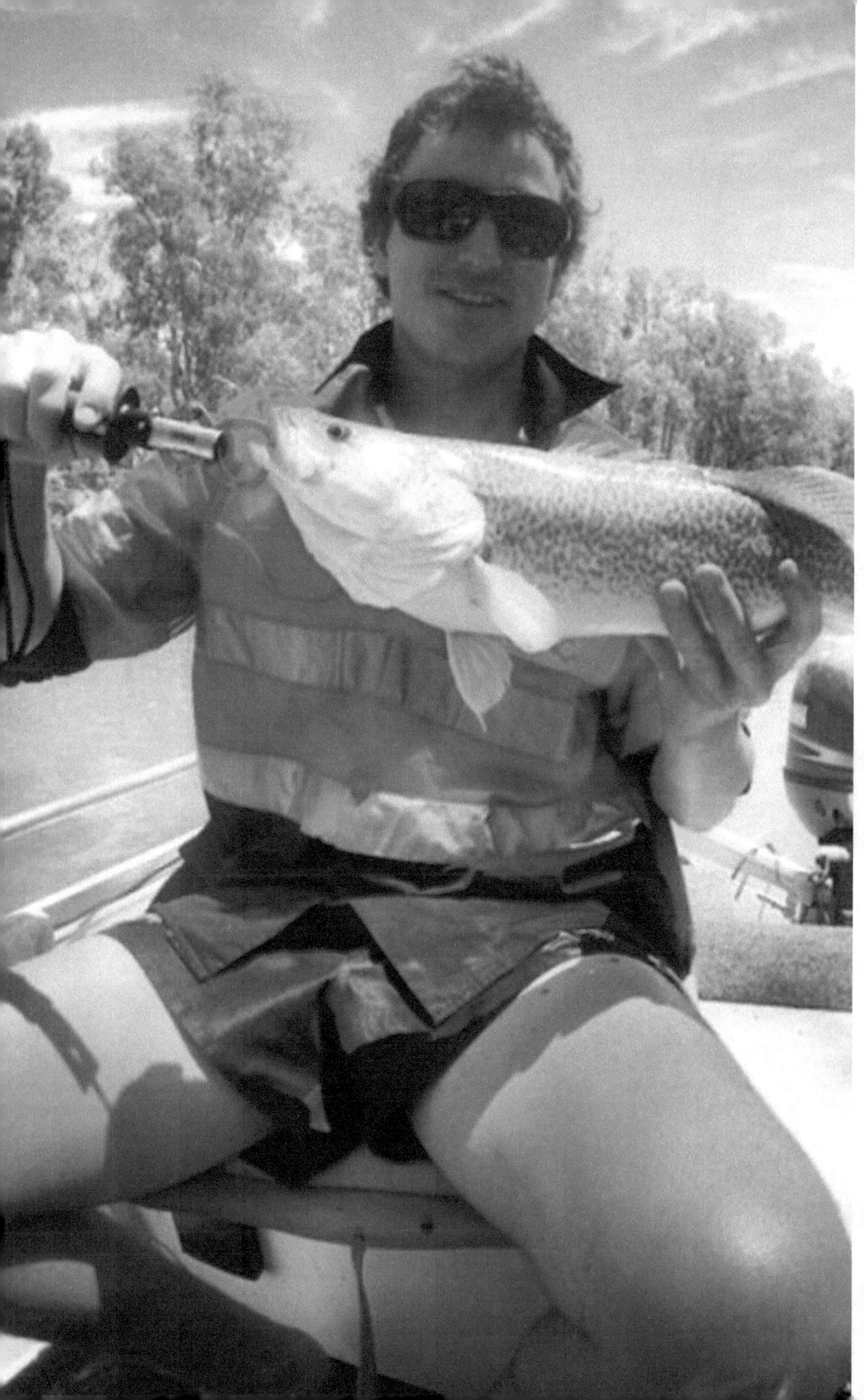

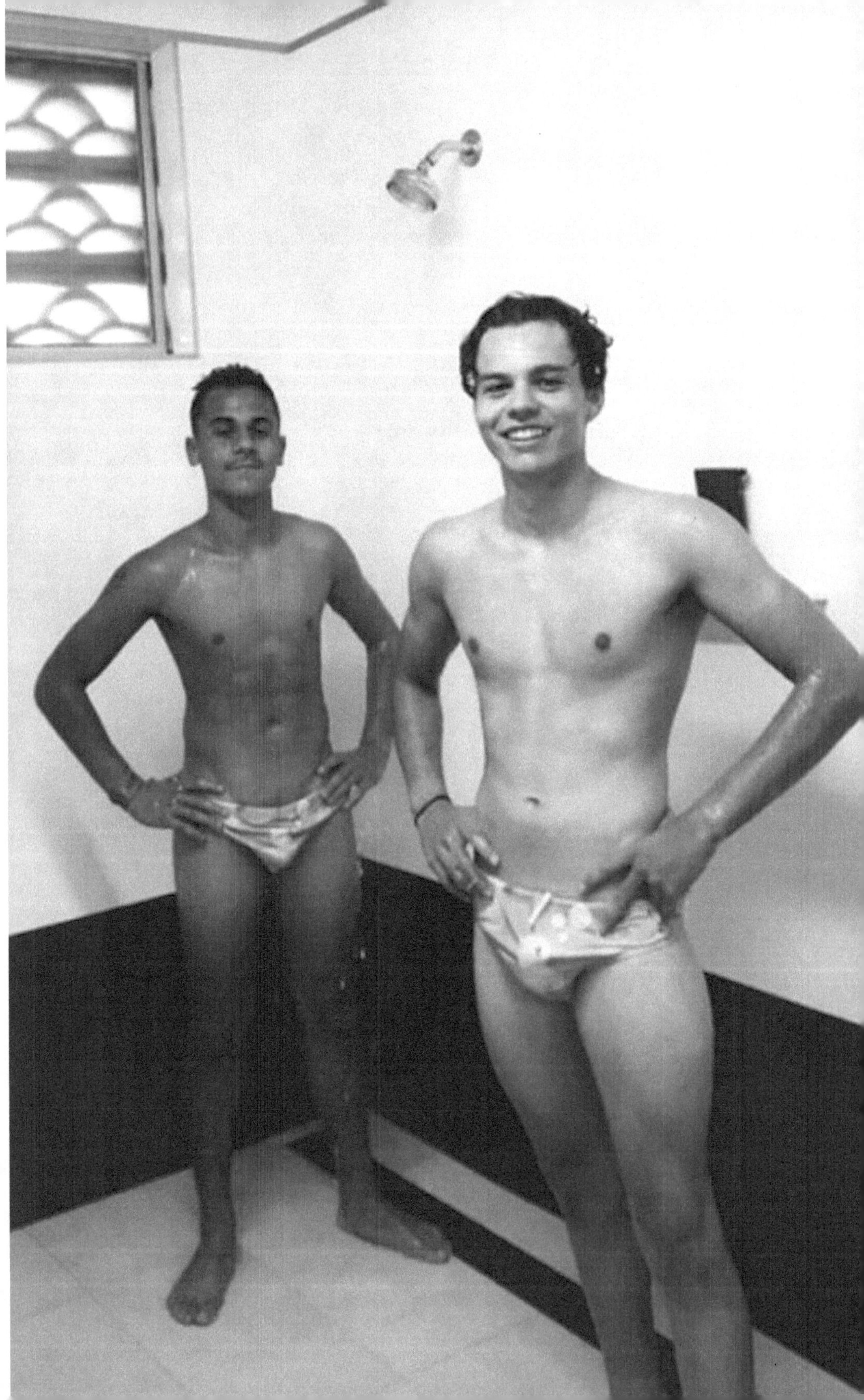

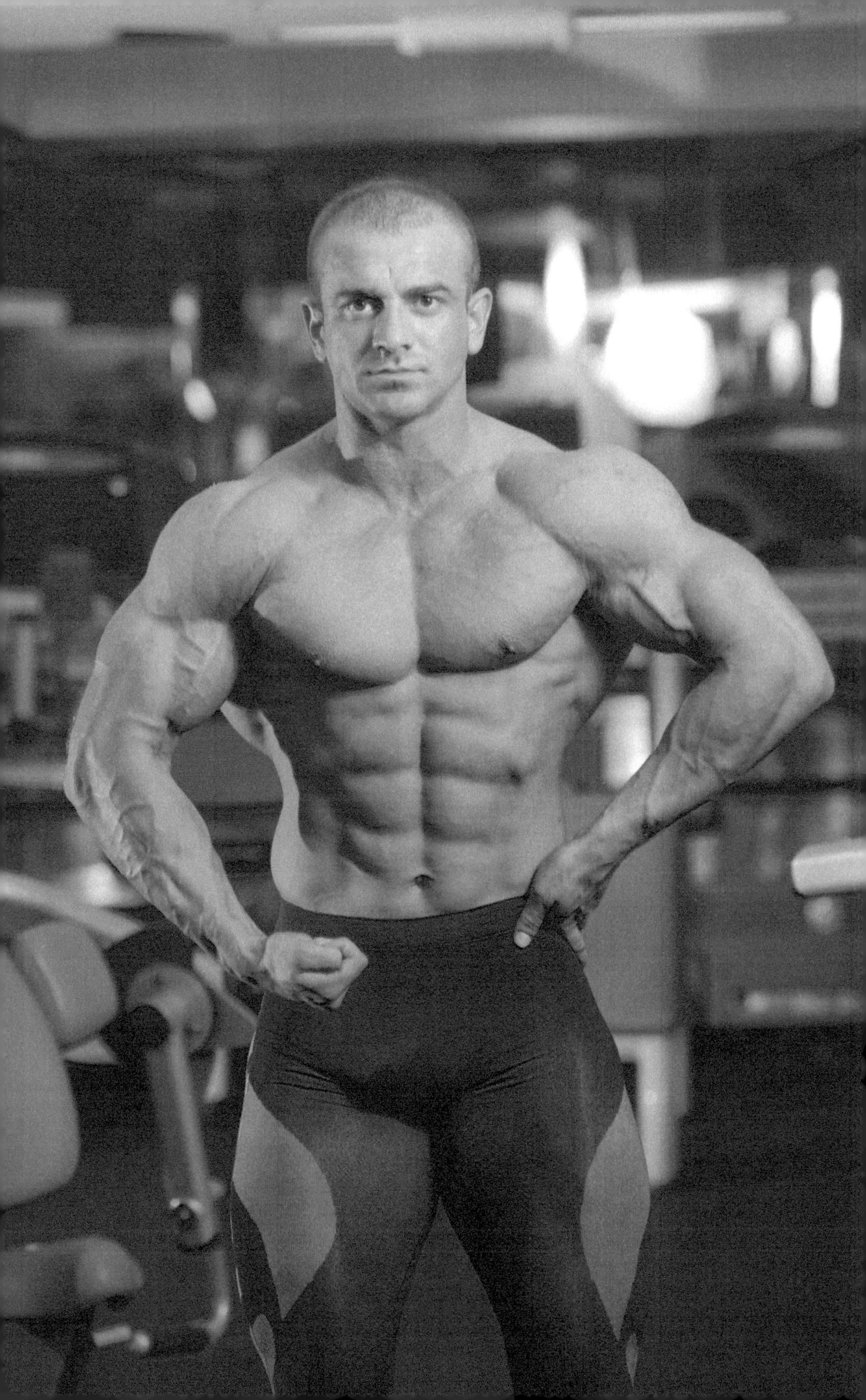

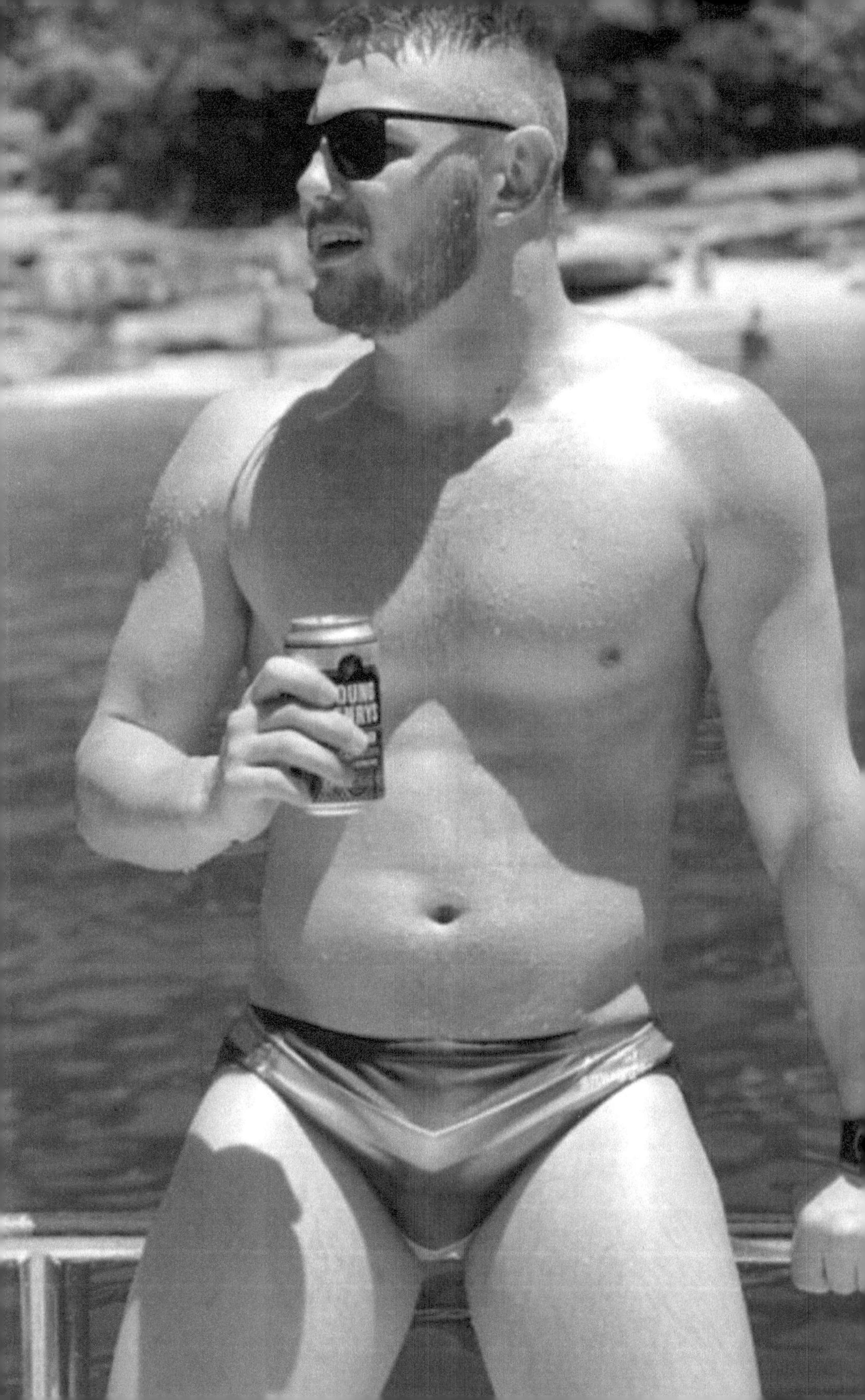

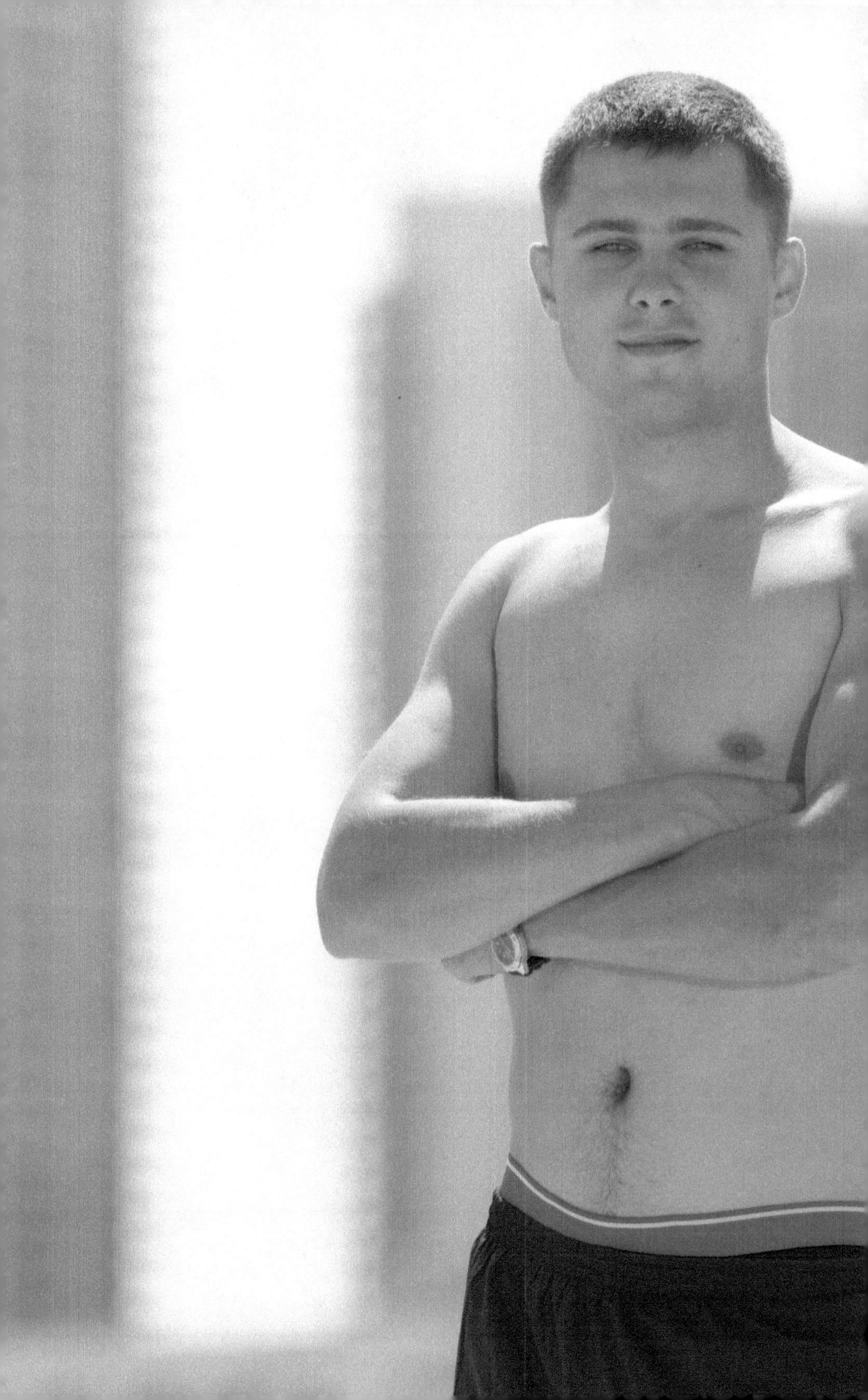

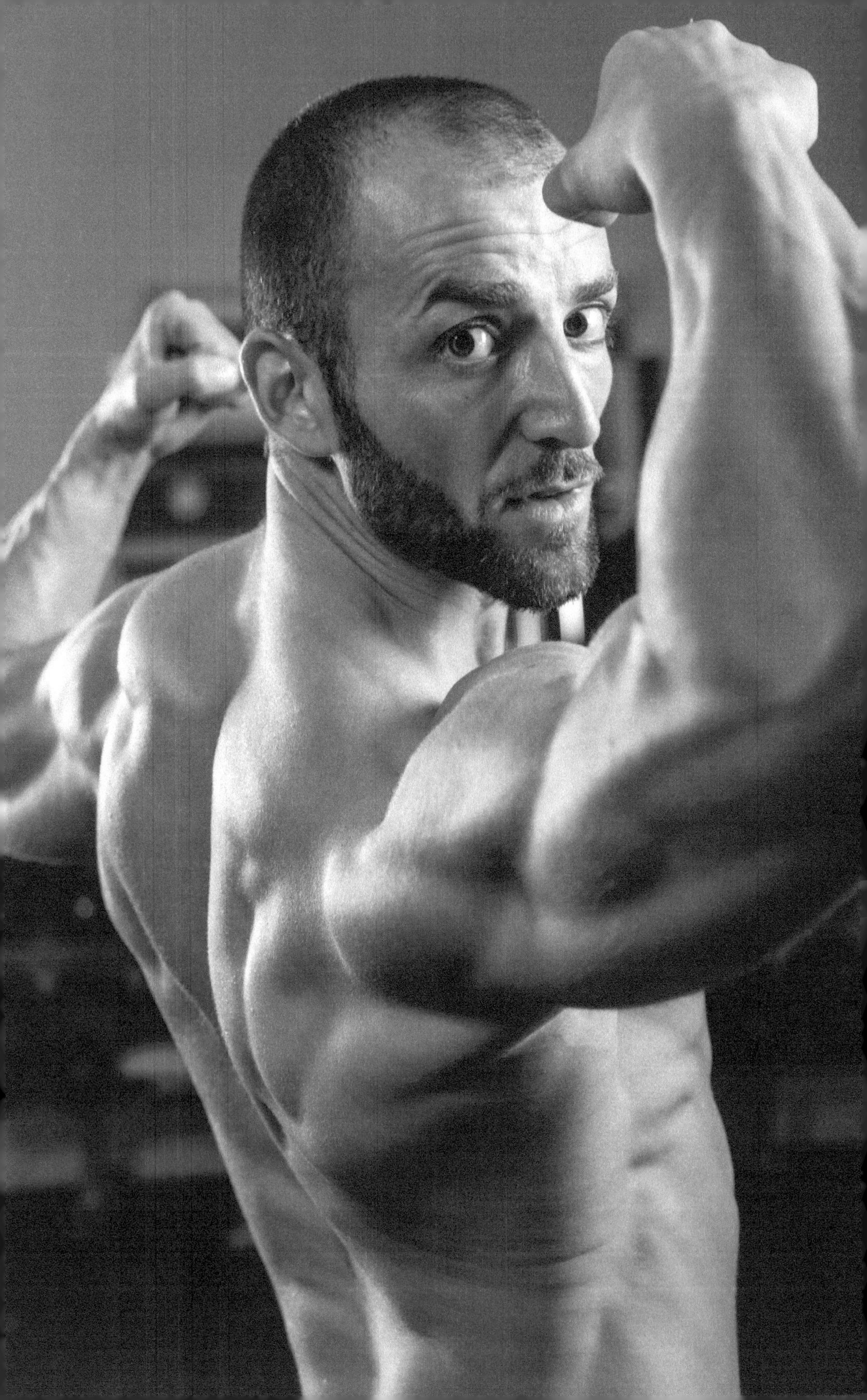

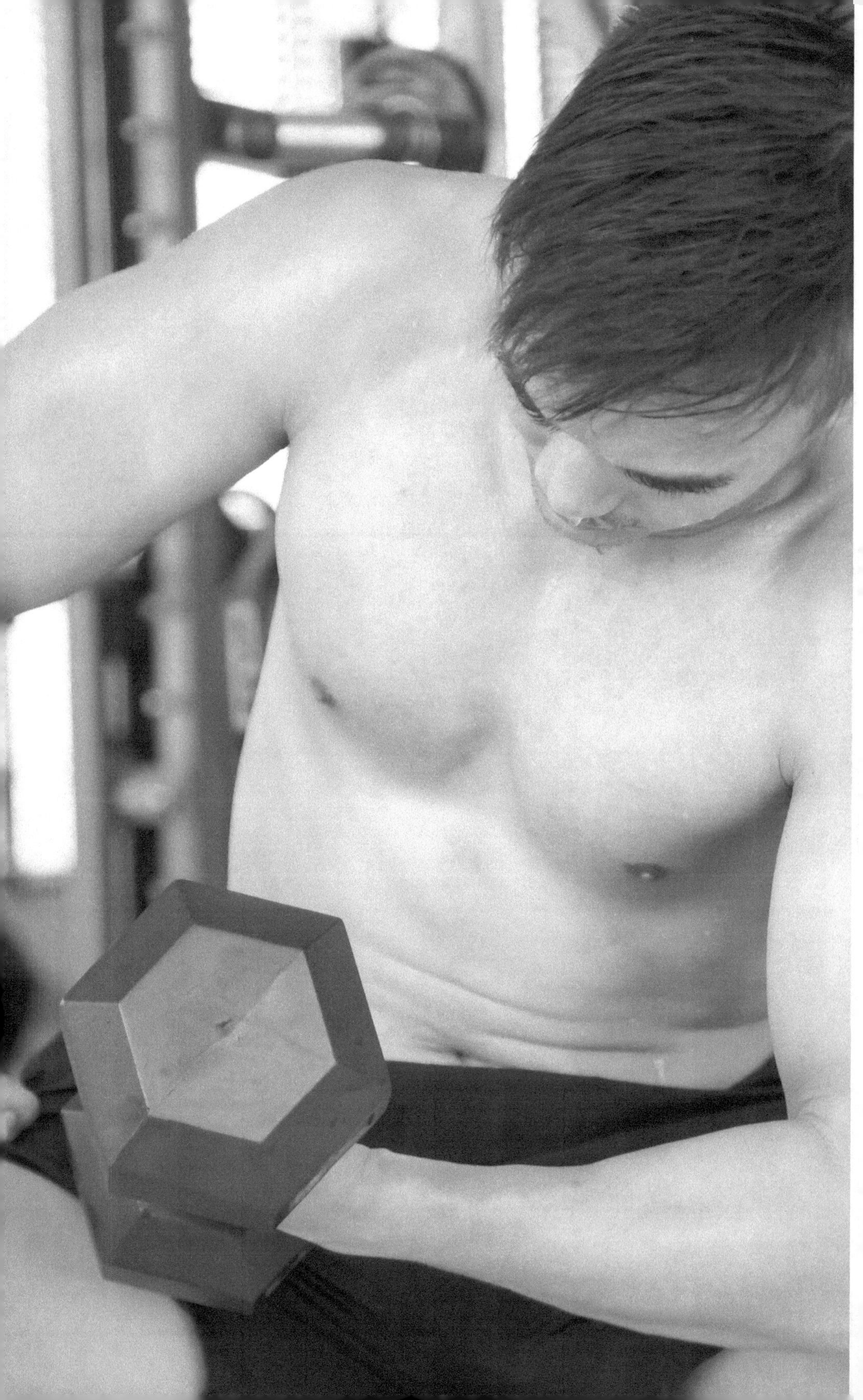

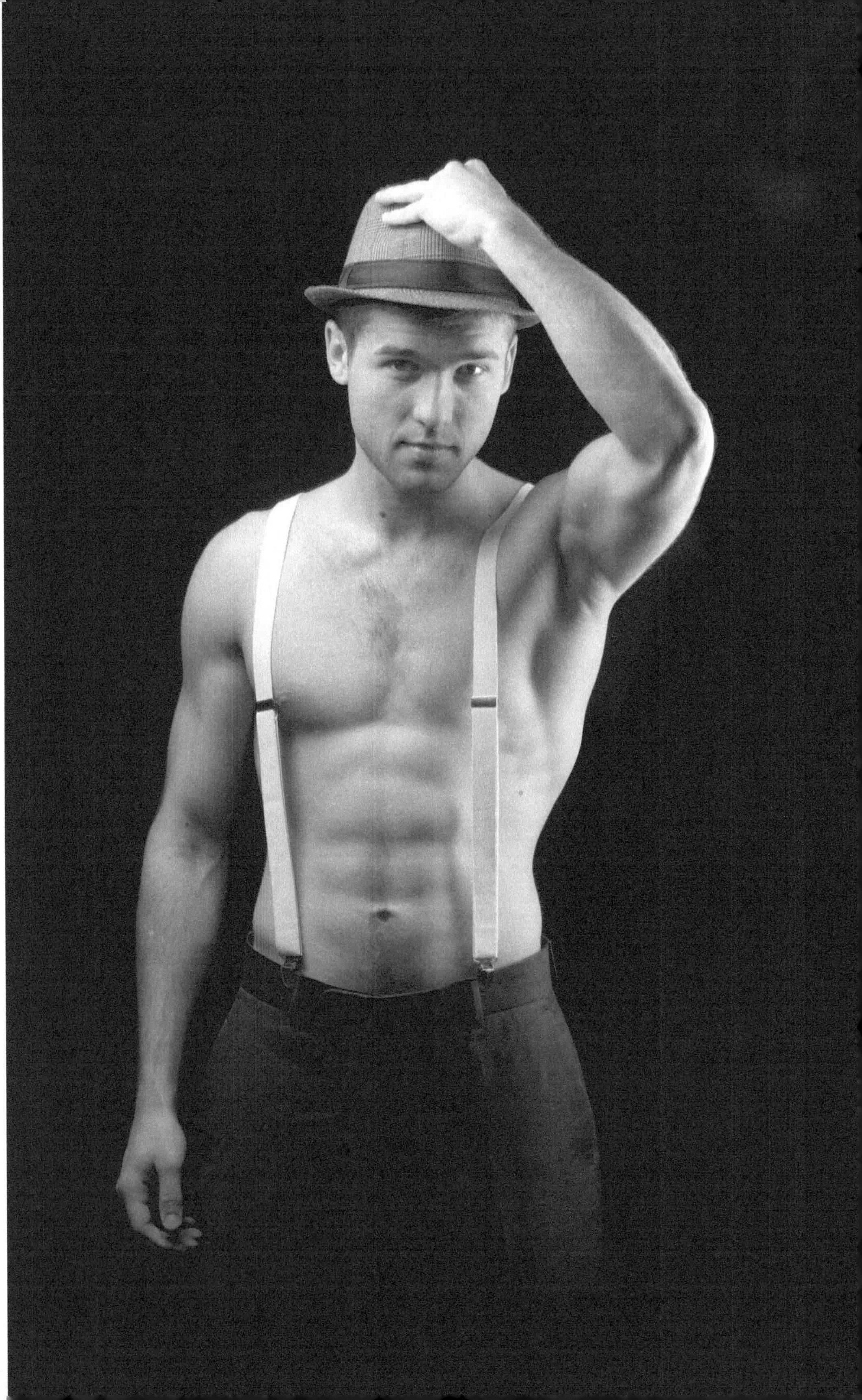

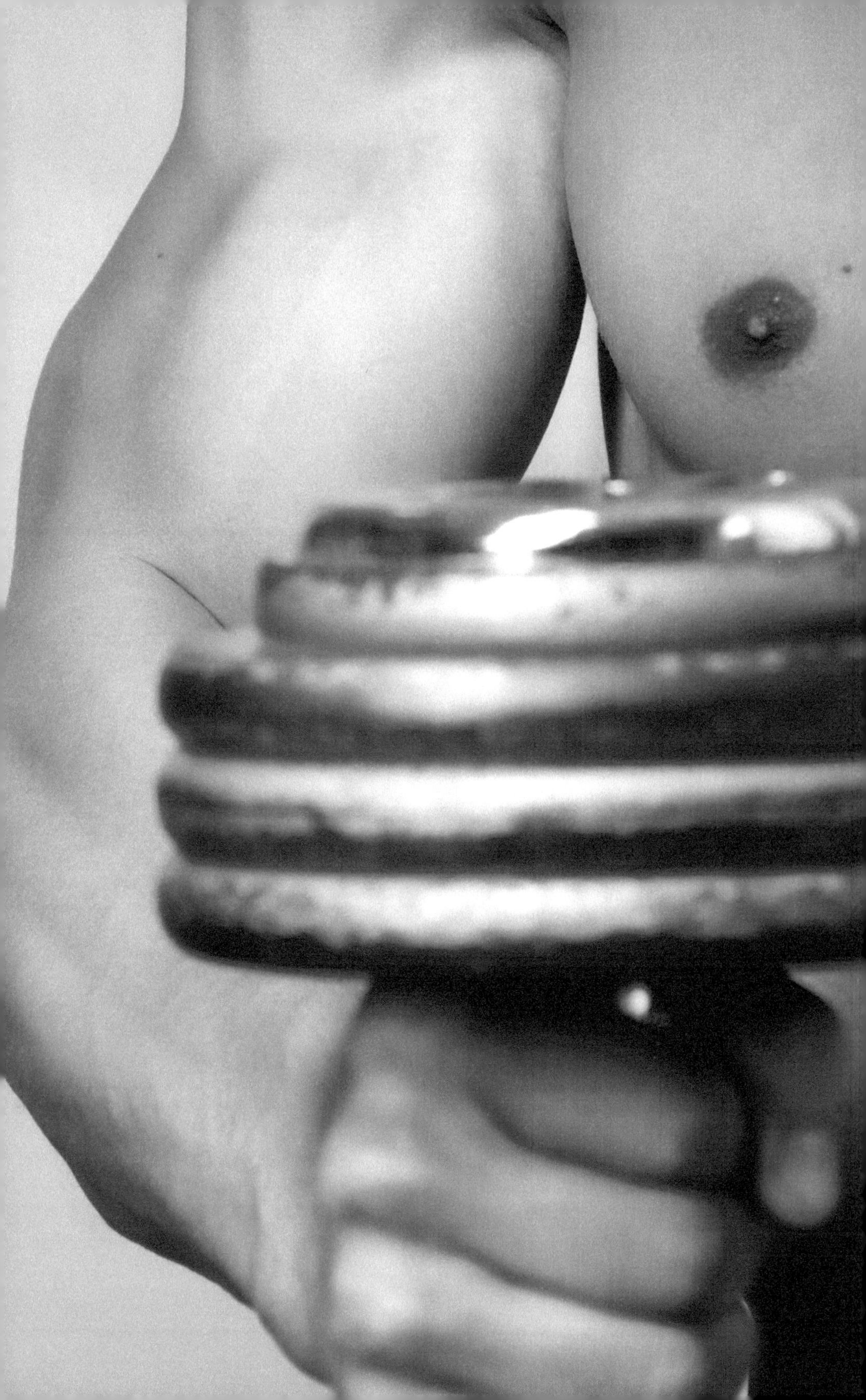

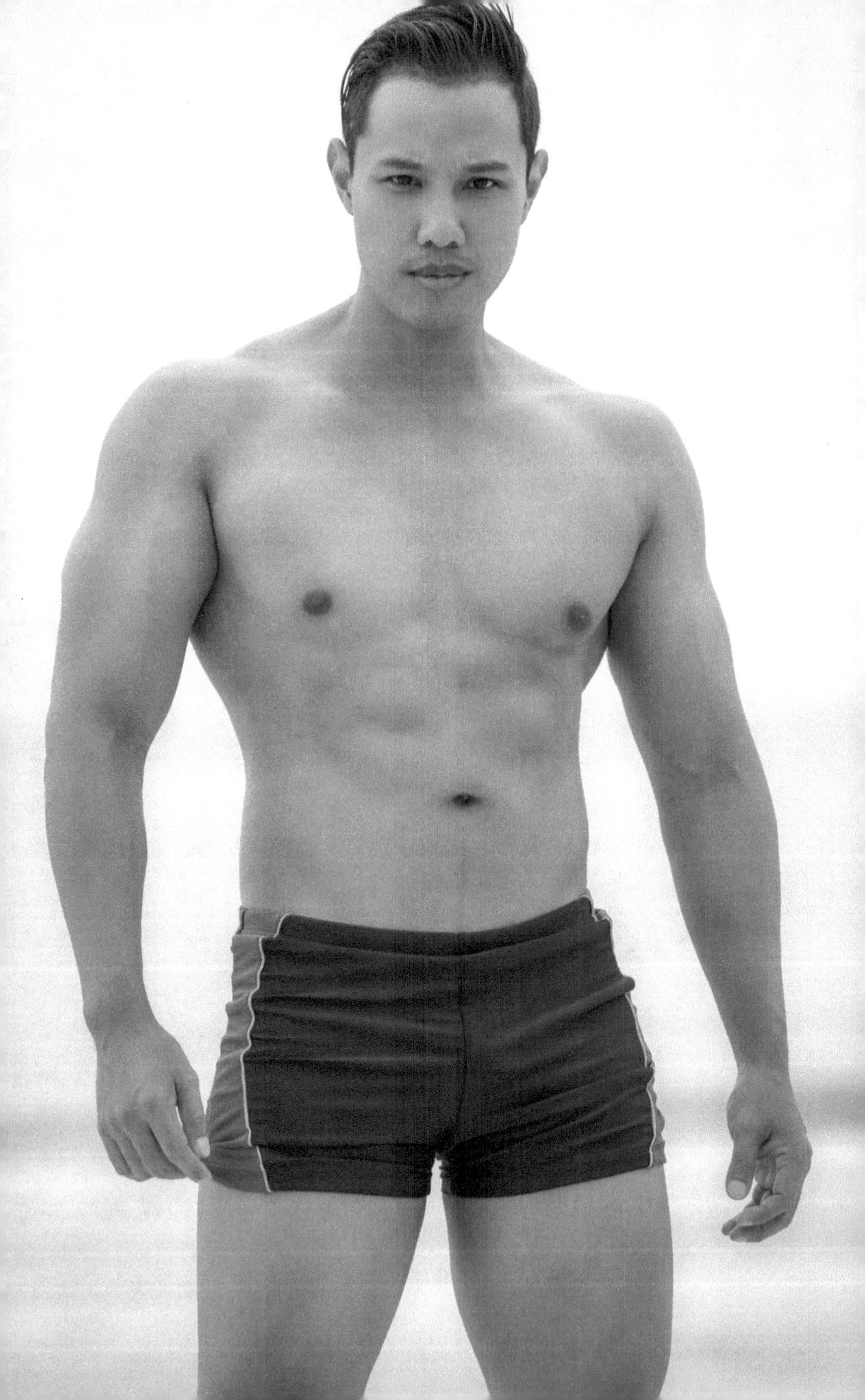

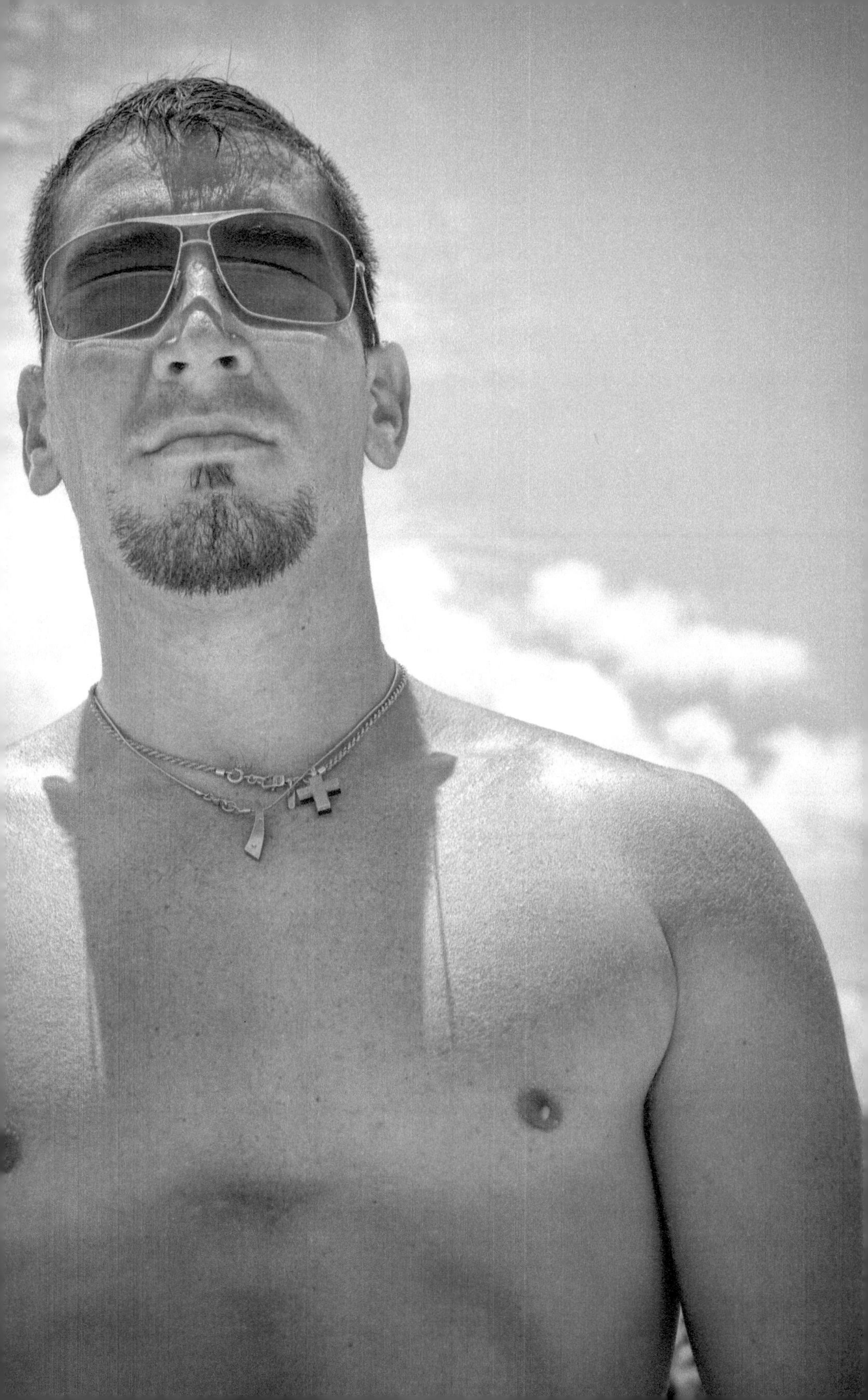

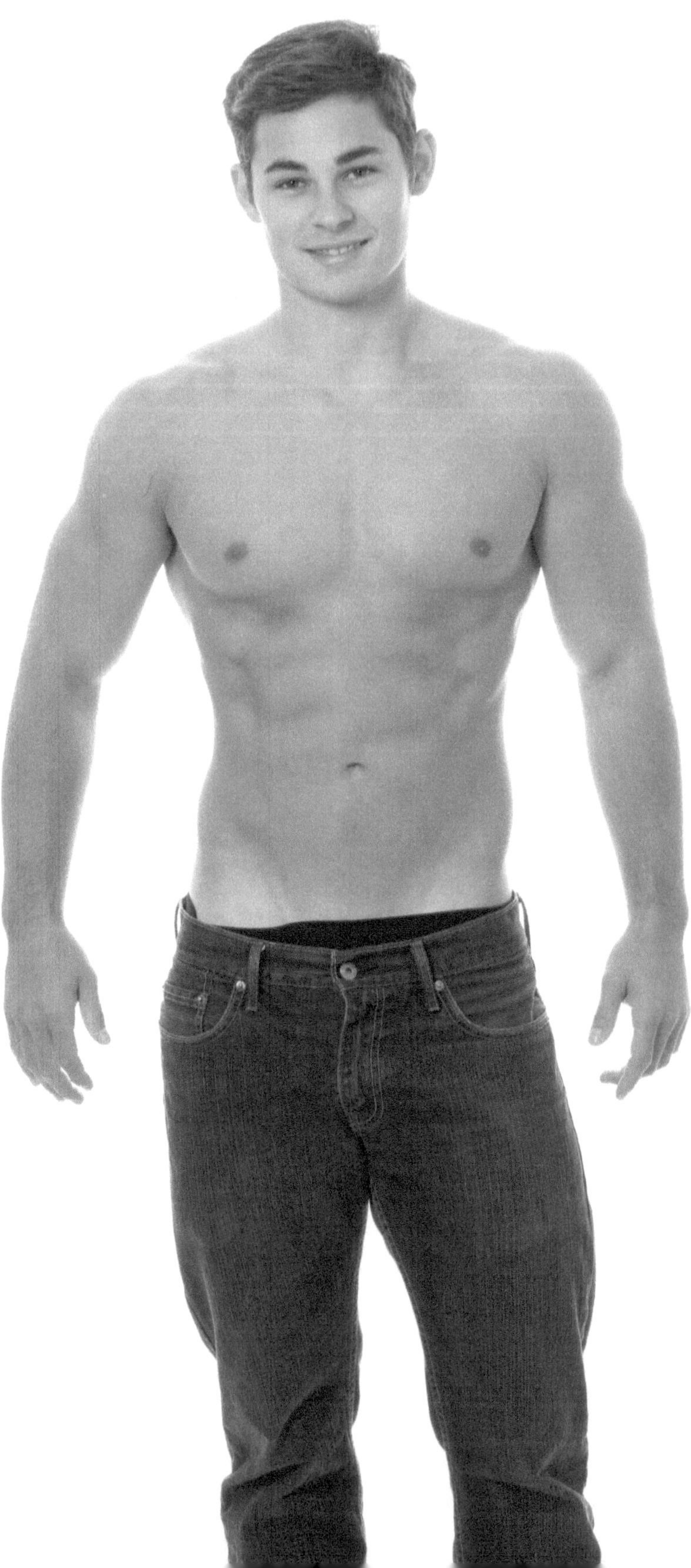

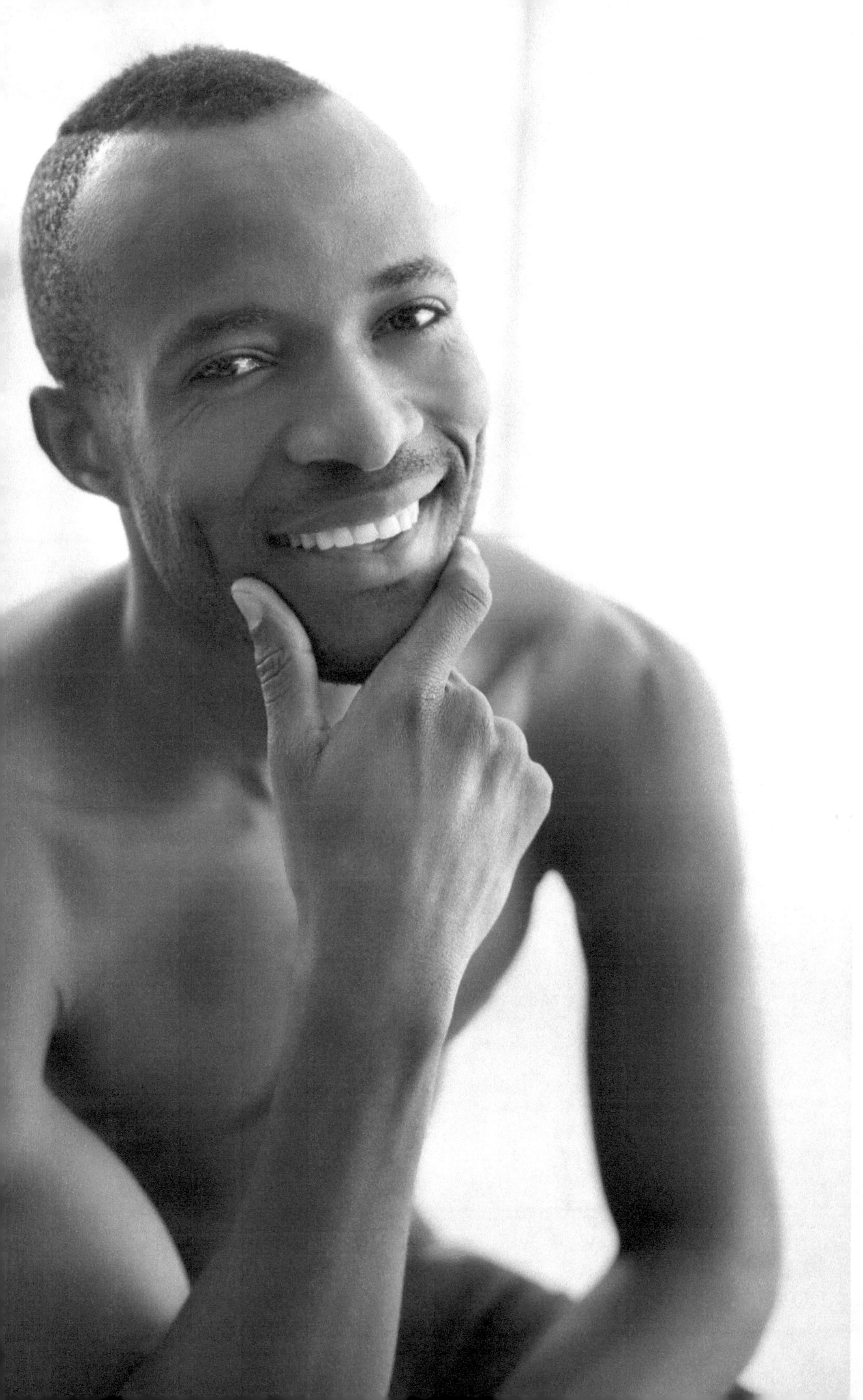

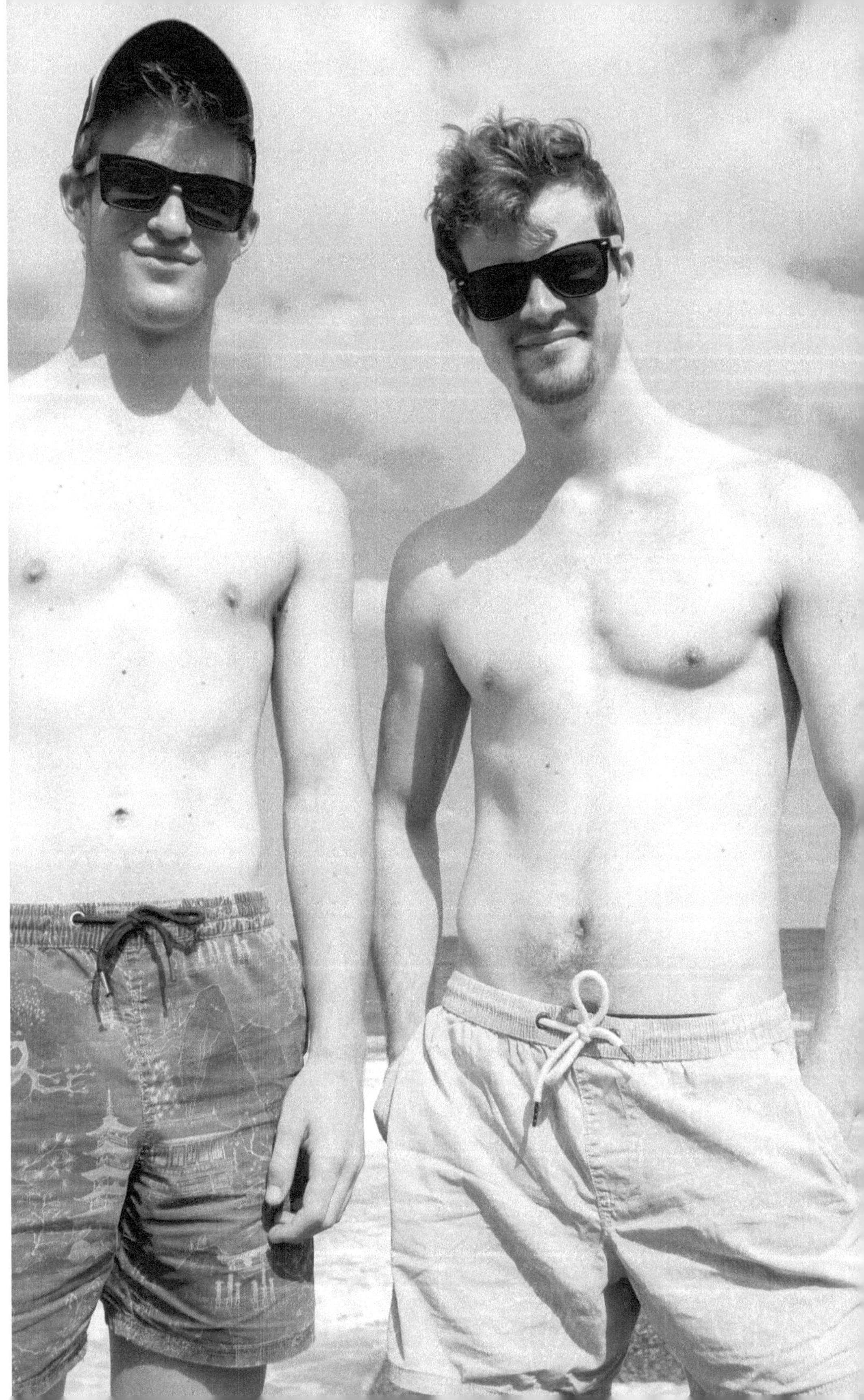

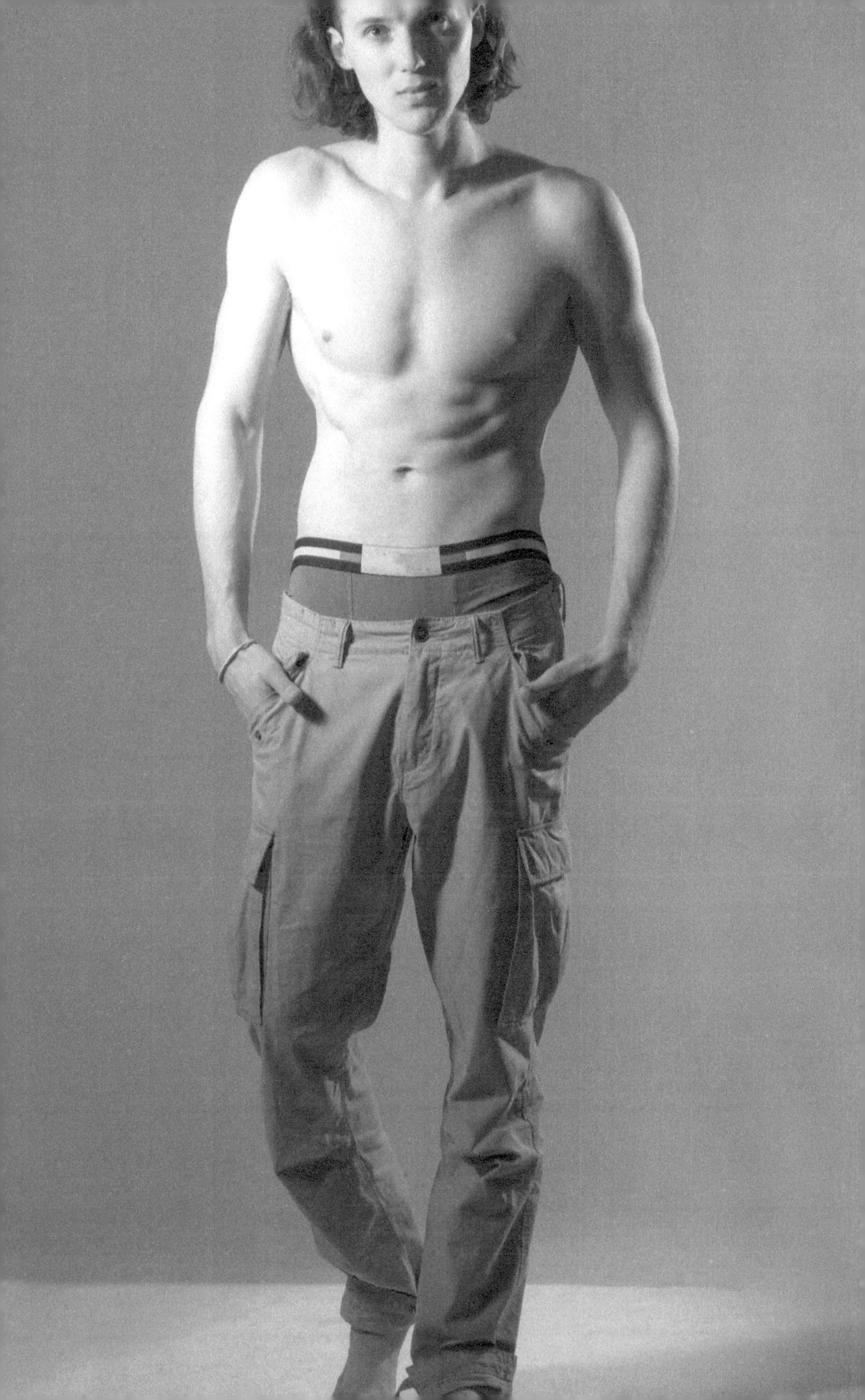

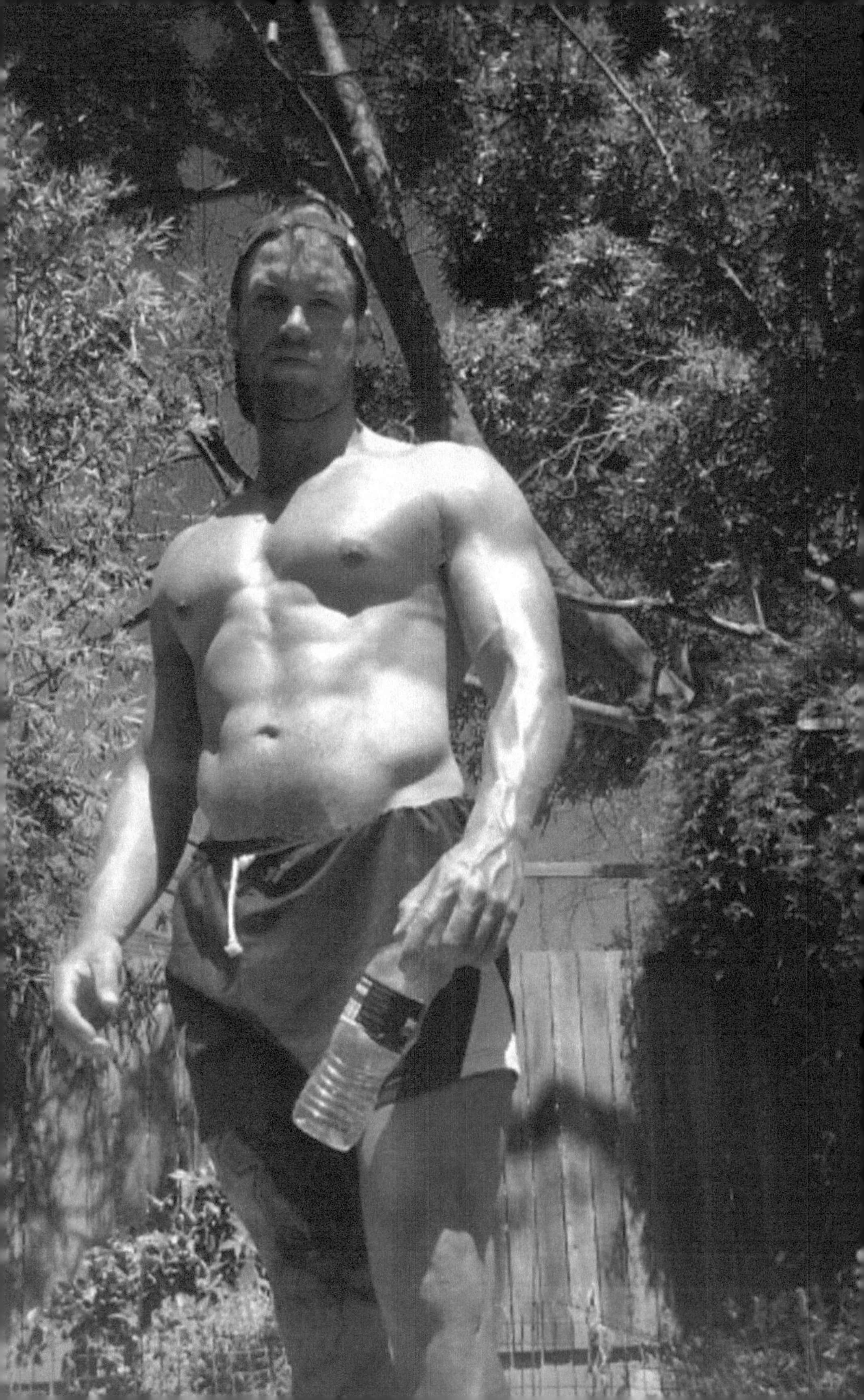

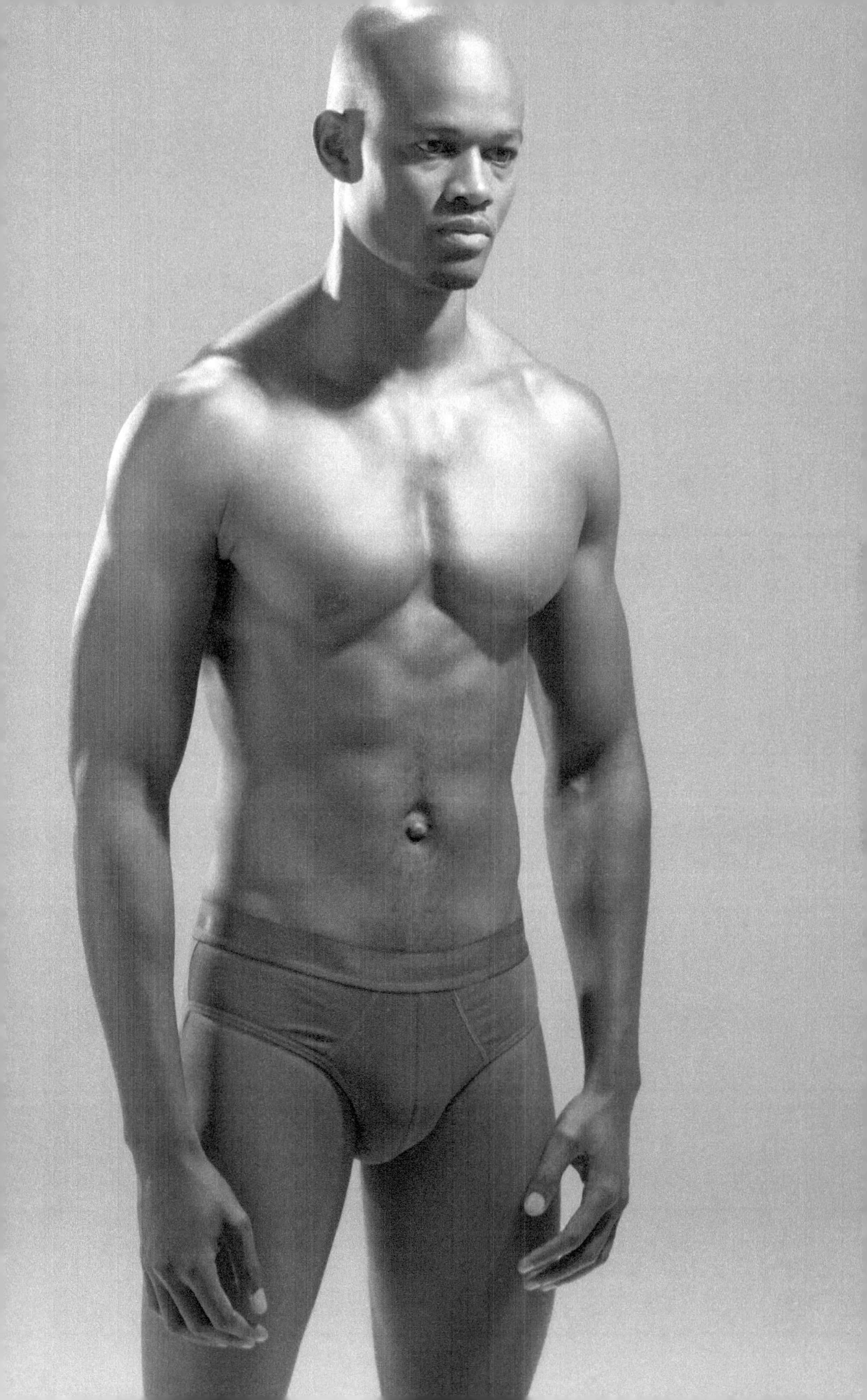

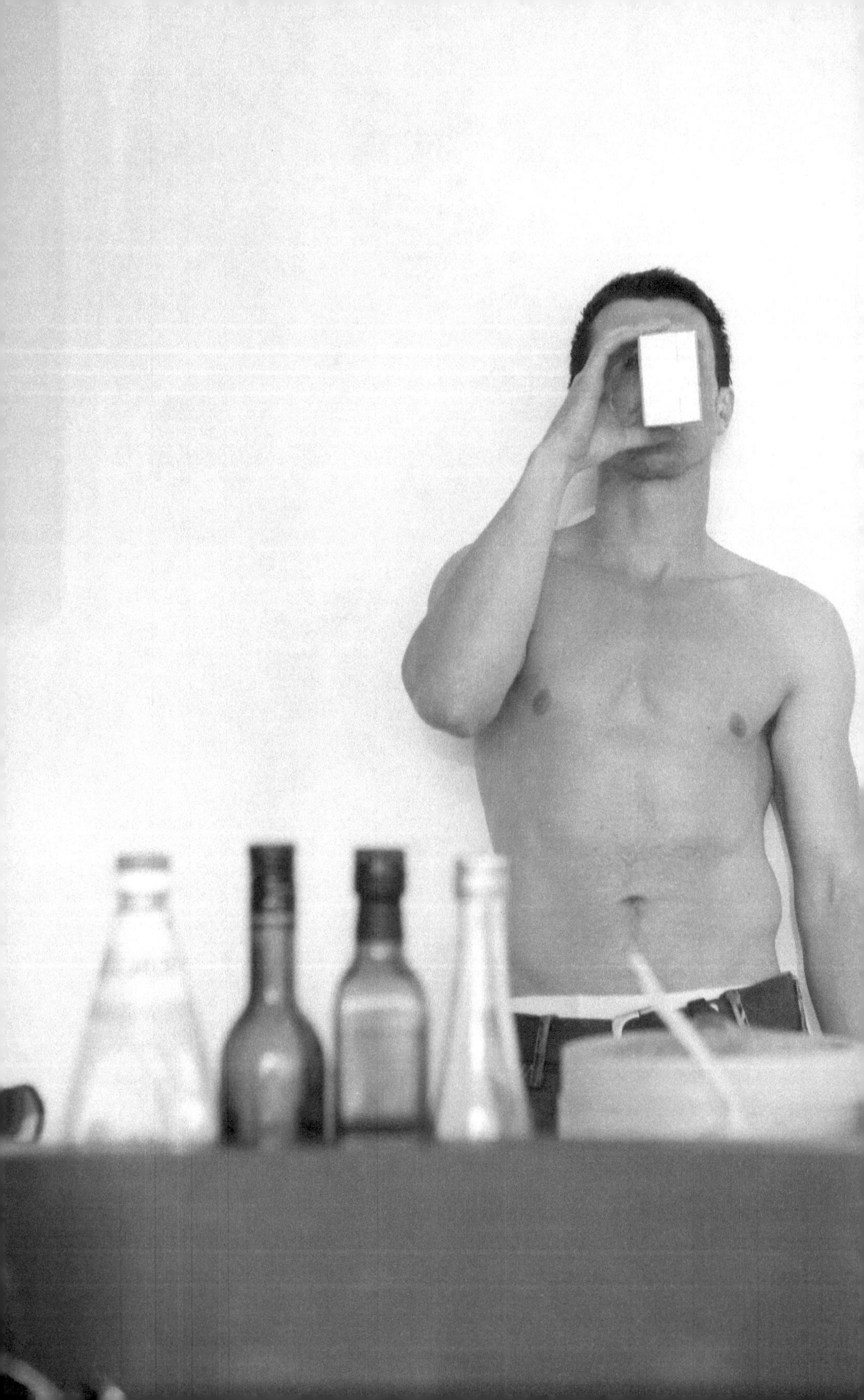

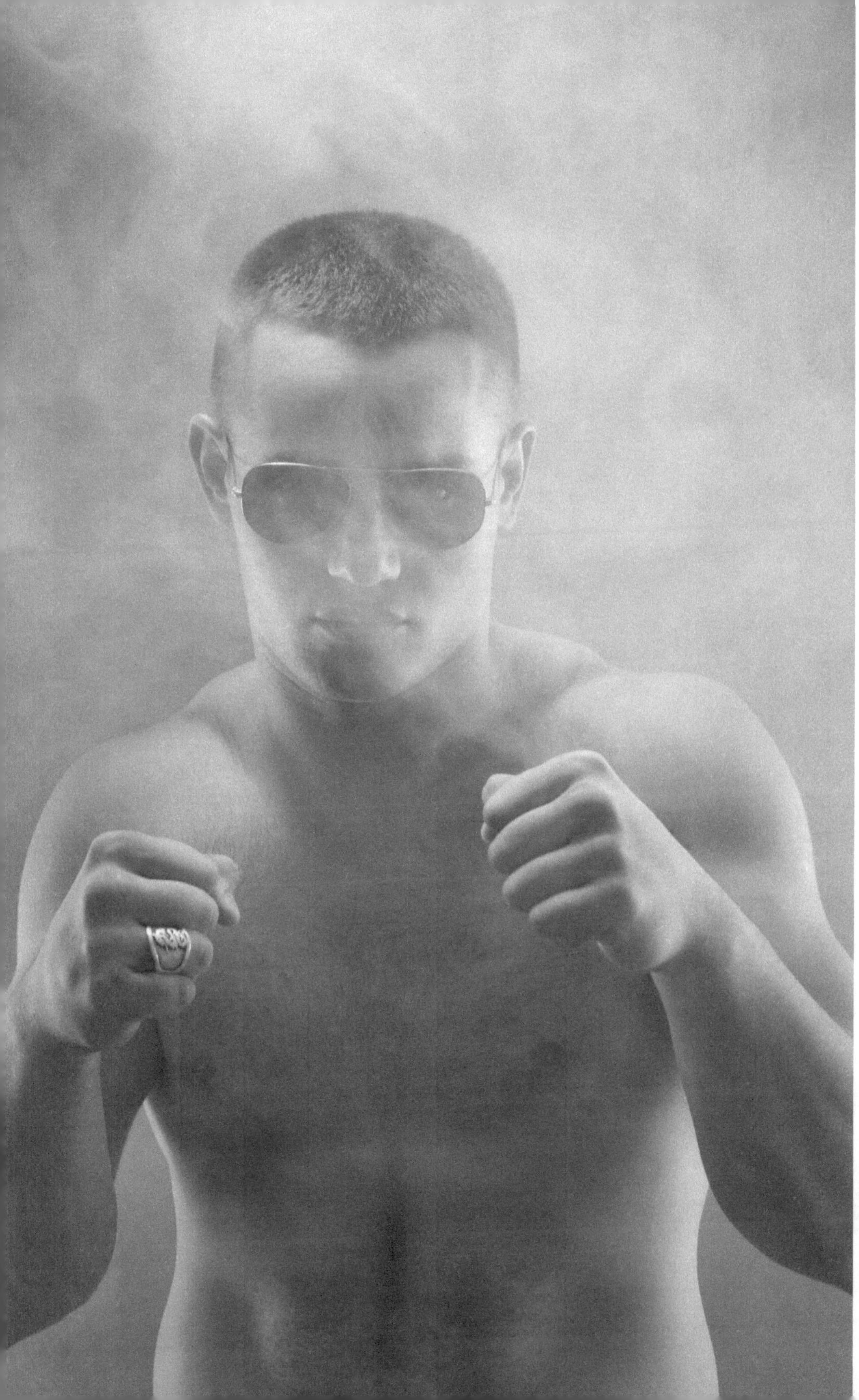

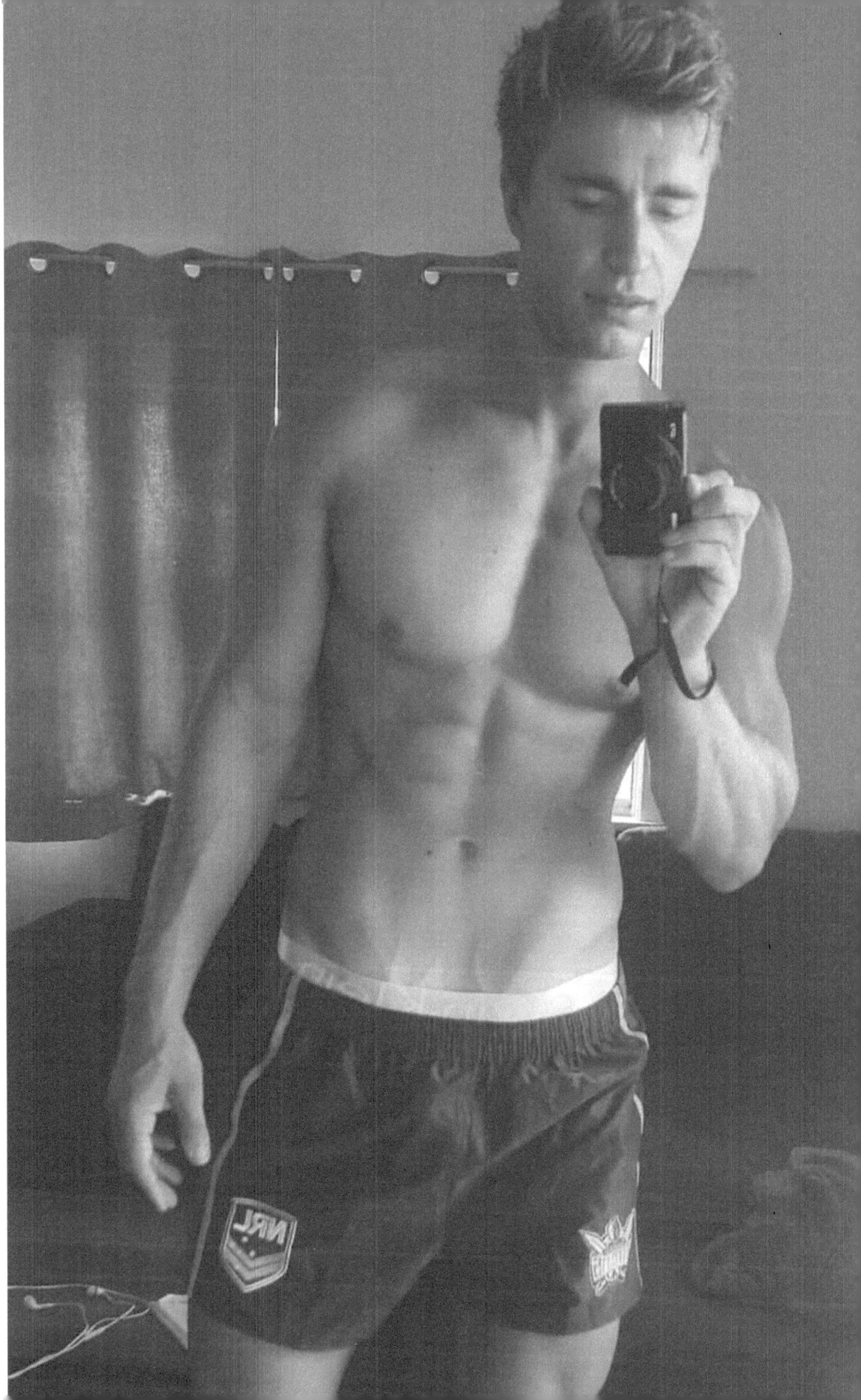

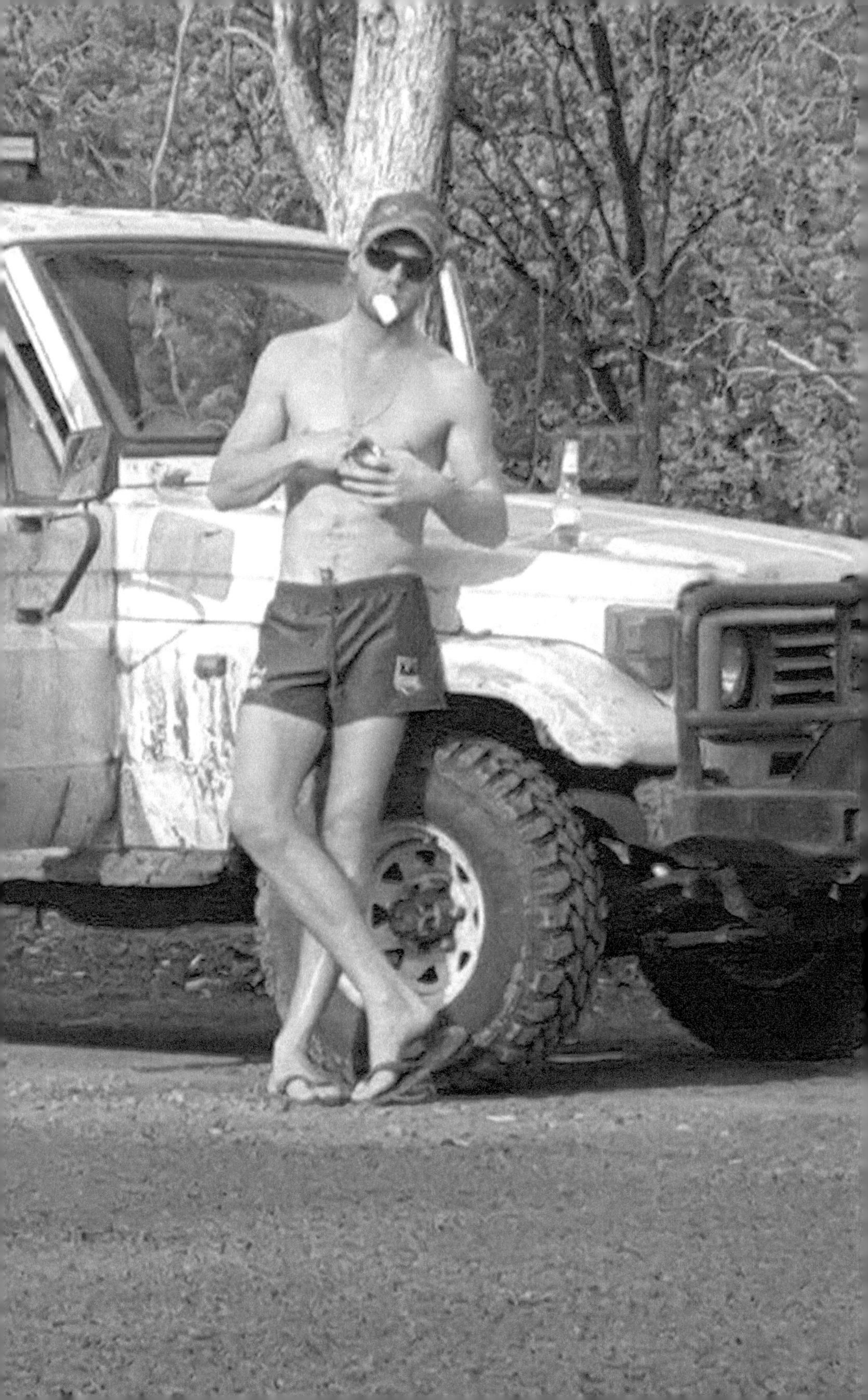

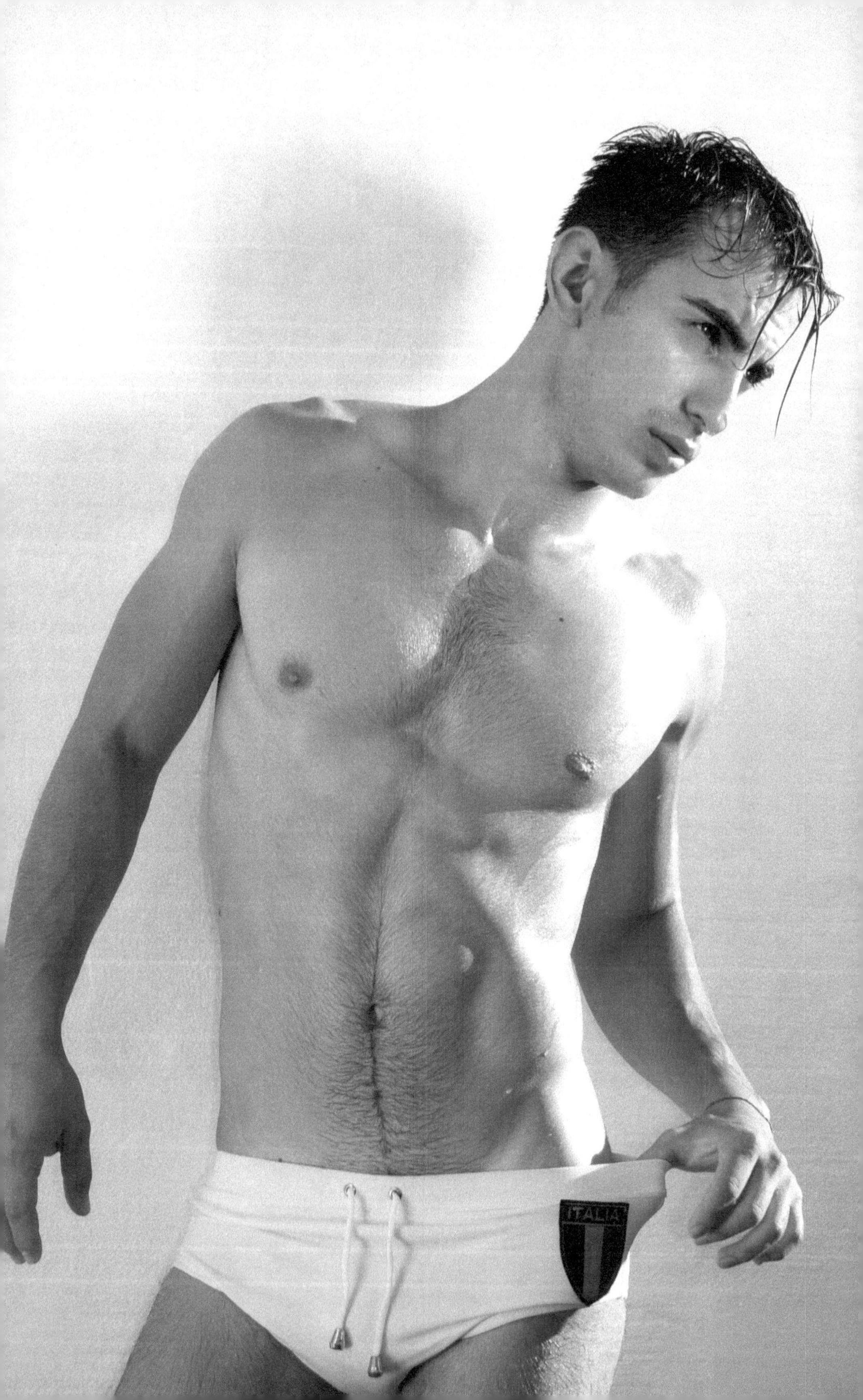
ITALIA

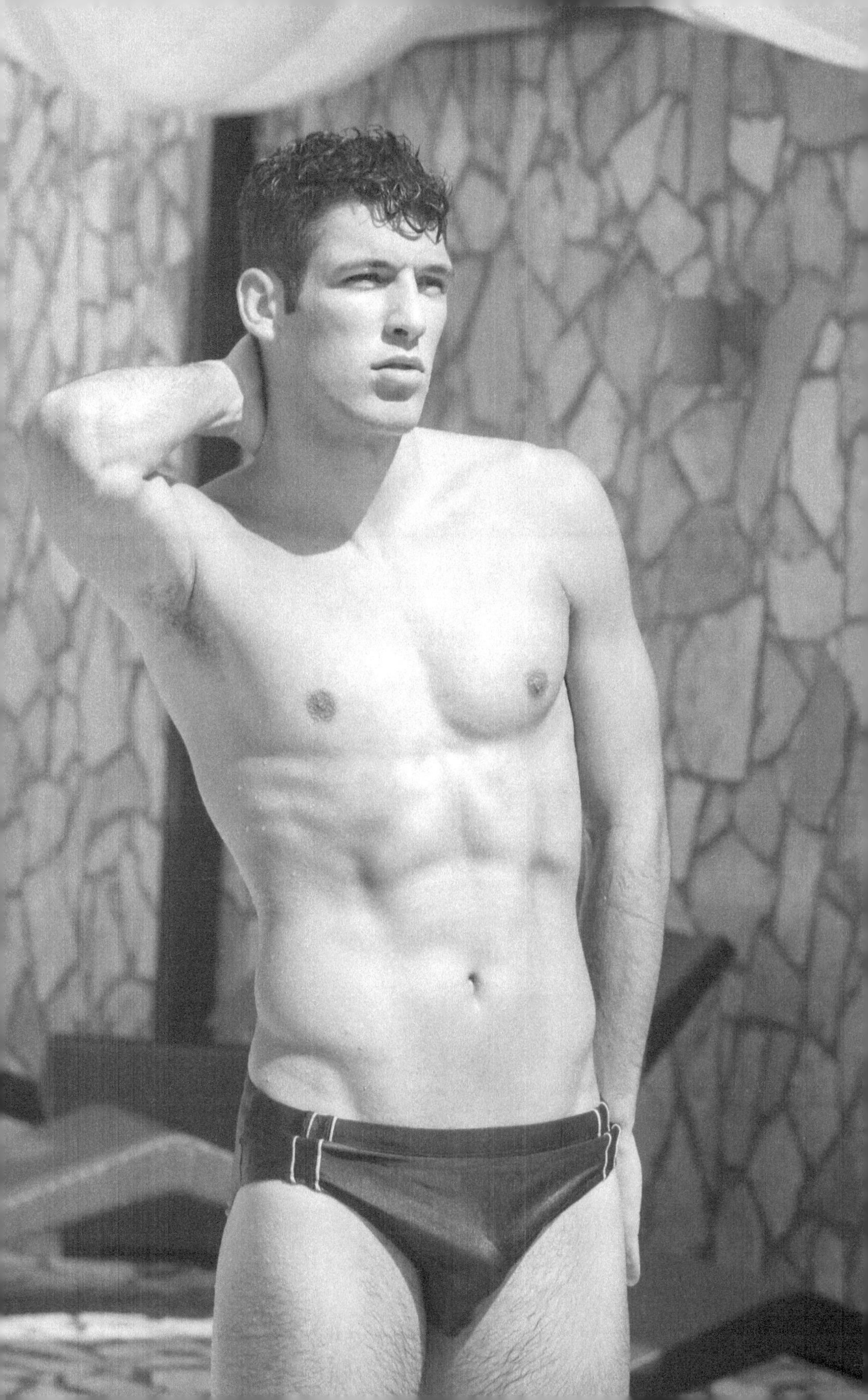

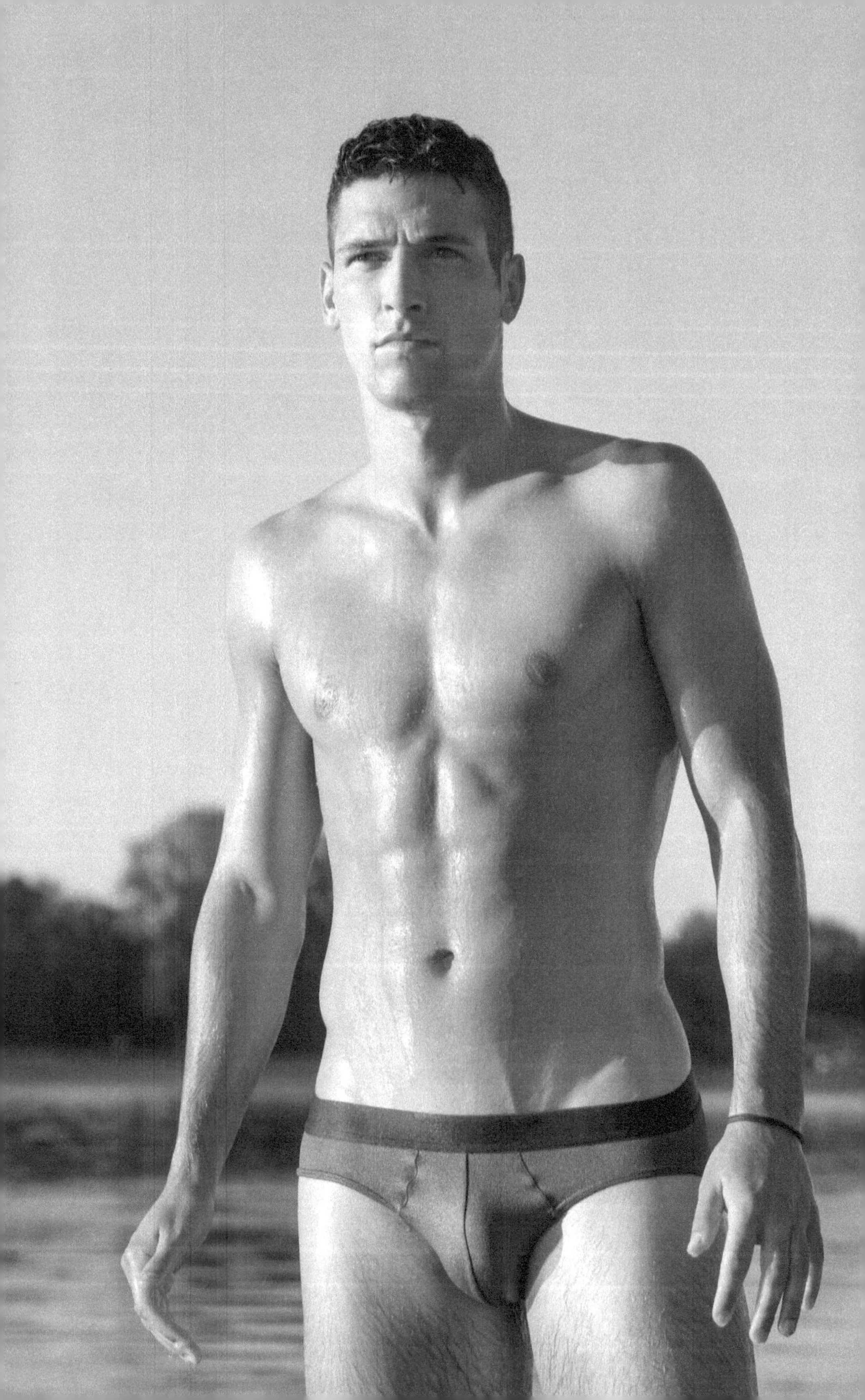

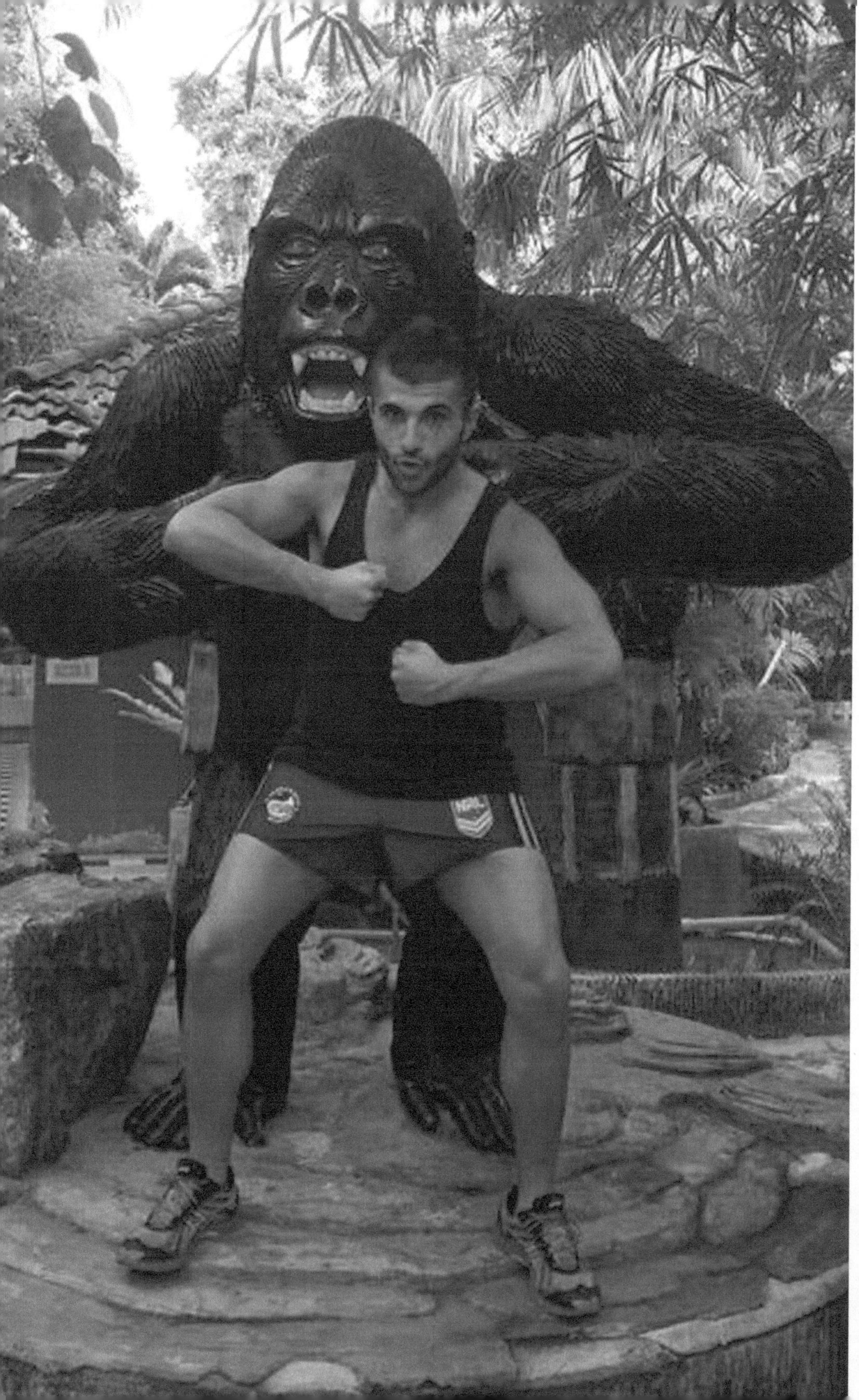

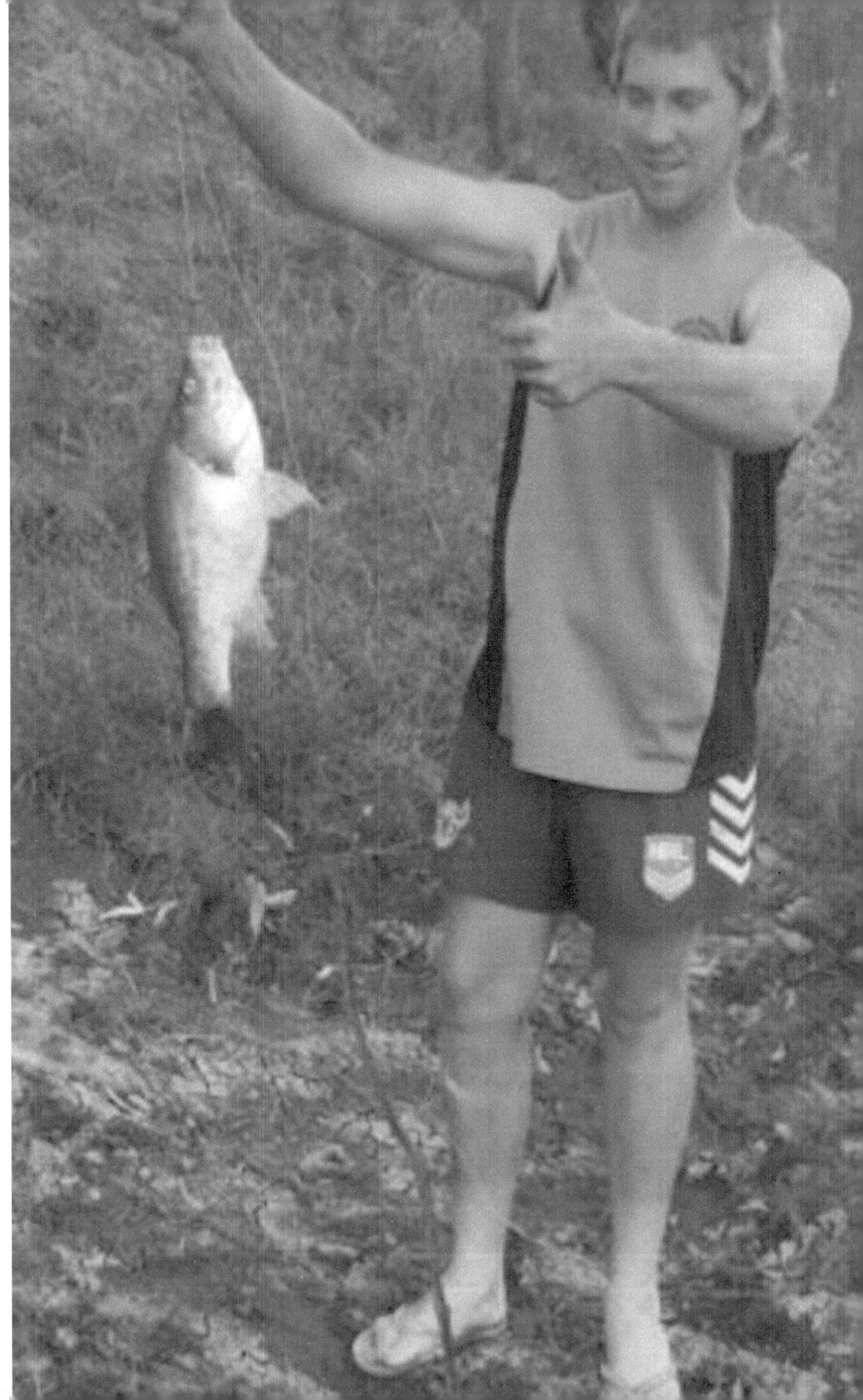

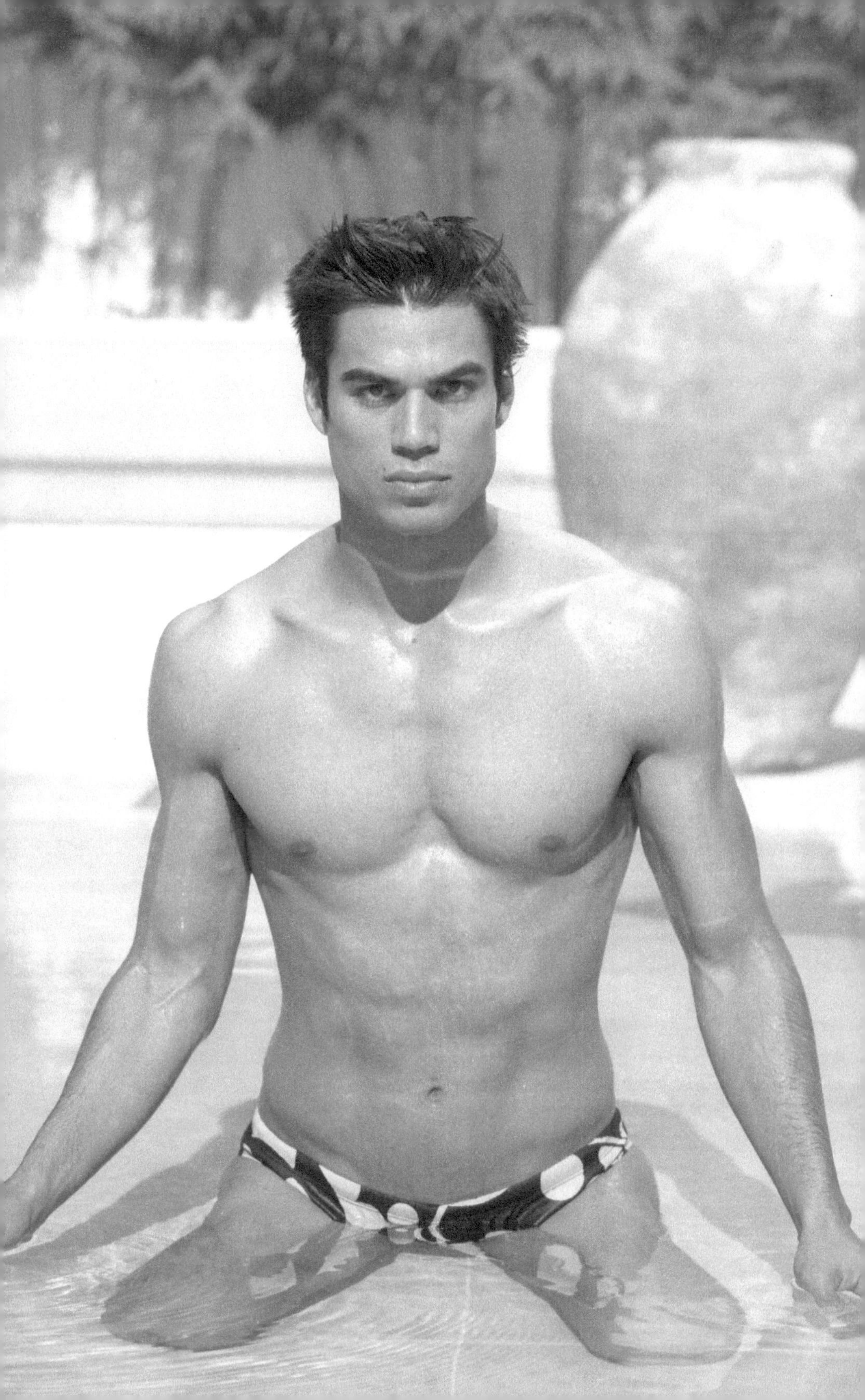

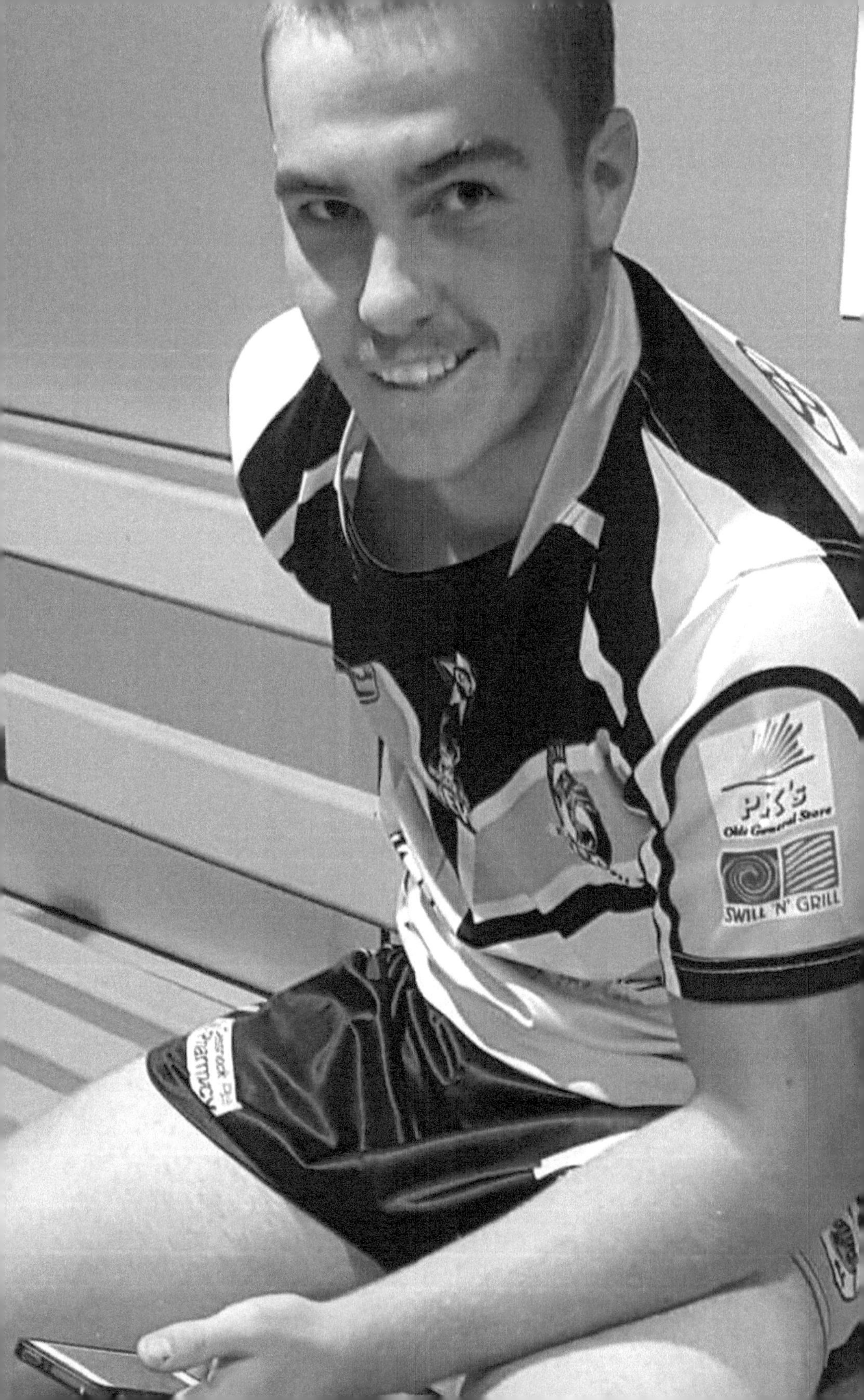
PK's
SWILL 'N' GRILL

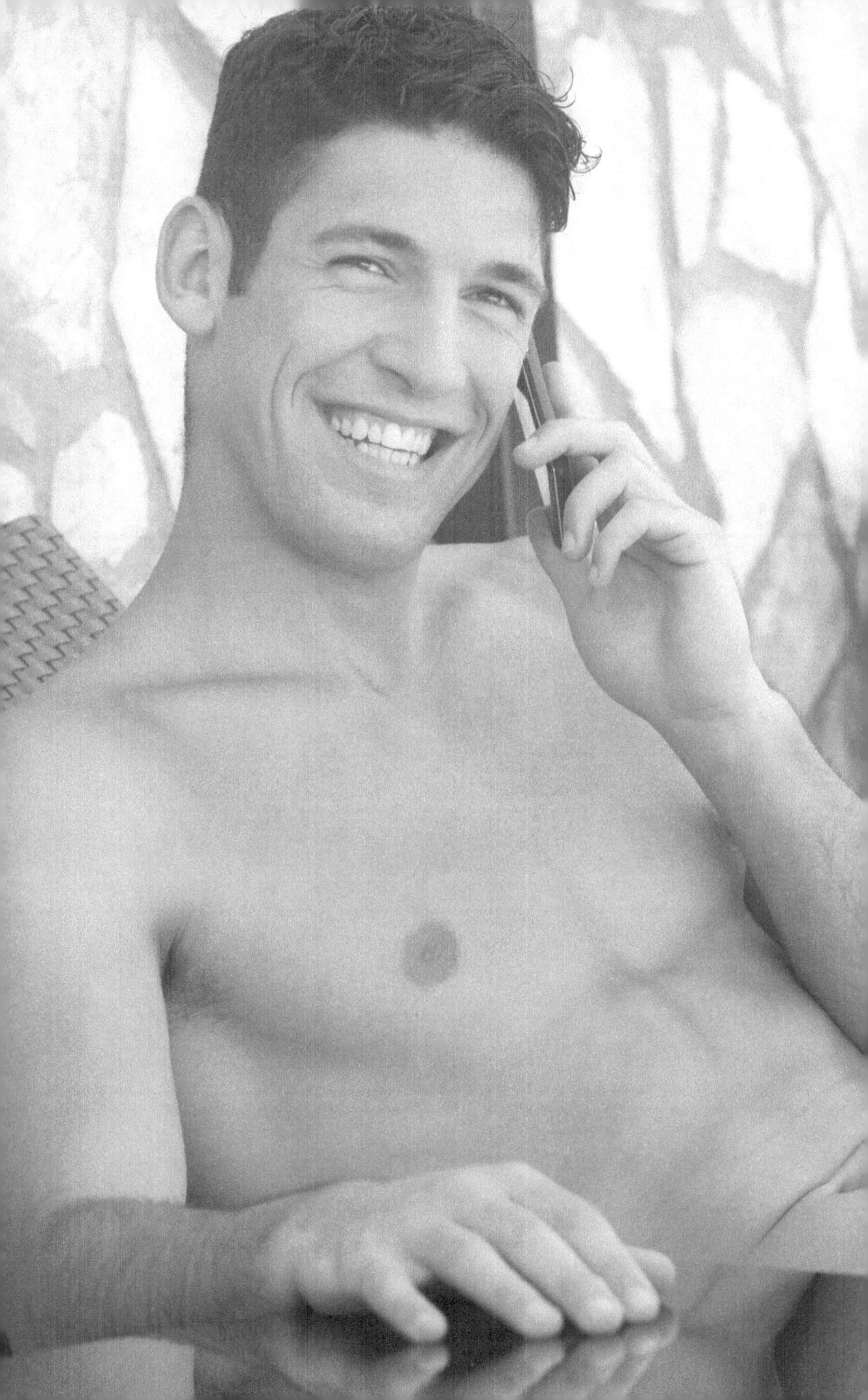

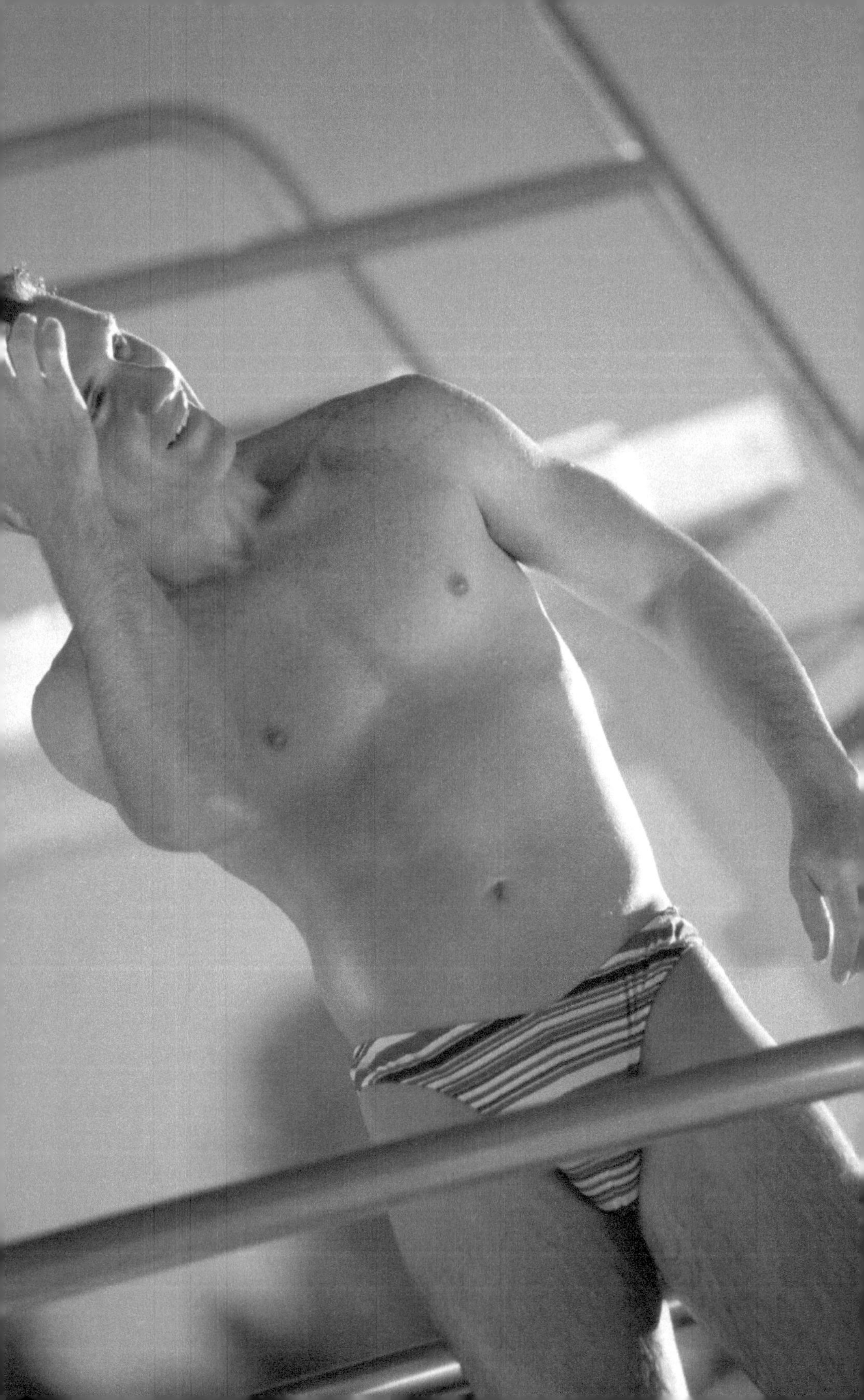

www.ingramcontent.com/pod-product-compliance
Lightning Source LLC
Chambersburg PA
CBHW021024180526
…53CB00005B/2100
9780359955312